CONTENTS

D1458982

PART FOUR
CRITICAL HISTORY

PART FIVE
BACKGROUND

PART ONE

INTRODUCTION

HOW TO STUDY A NOVEL

Studying a novel on your own requires self-discipline and a carefully thought-out work plan in order to be effective.

- You will need to read the novel more than once. Start by reading it quickly for pleasure, then read it slowly and thoroughly.

- On your second reading make detailed notes on the plot, characters and themes of the novel. Further readings will generate new ideas and help you to memorise the details of the story.

- Some of the characters will develop as the plot unfolds. How do your responses towards them change during the course of the novel?

- Think about how the novel is narrated. From whose point of view are events described?

- A novel may or may not present events chronologically: the time-scheme may be a key to its structure and organisation.

- What part do the settings play in the novel?

- Are words, images or incidents repeated so as to give the work a pattern? Do such patterns help you to understand the novel's themes?

- Identify what styles of language are used in the novel.

- What is the effect of the novel's ending? Is the action completed and closed, or left incomplete and open?

- Does the novel present a moral and just world?

- Cite exact sources for all quotations, whether from the text itself or from critical commentaries. Wherever possible find your own examples from the novel to back up your opinions.

- Always express your ideas in your own words.

These York Notes offer an introduction to *Wuthering Heights* and cannot substitute for close reading of the text and the study of secondary sources.

CHECK THE BOOK

Wuthering Heights will generously reward attentive readers yielding far more enriching insights than any secondary sources, which should always invite you back to the original text.

CONTEXT

In the nineteenth century, it was usual to regard novels as a personal and privileged communication from the author to the reader, rather like a confidence or a message. Given this critical environment, even the critics who acknowledged the power of this book found it rude and disturbing. Victorian readers believed that the purpose of literature was to understand man and his capabilities. *Wuthering Heights* seemed like an affront, and it confounded all their notions of what could or should constitute good literature.

READING *WUTHERING HEIGHTS*

Wuthering Heights is a highly provoking book, as the wealth of literary criticism devoted to Emily Brontë attests. From its earliest reception, Emily Brontë's only novel has excited intense debate amongst its critics and readers. Flouting the conventions of its day, it was initially reviewed, in January 1848, a month after its publication, in *Douglas Jerrold's Weekly Newspaper* as 'a strange sort of book – baffling all regular criticism'

However, by the early 1920s this response had altered dramatically. There were two main reasons for this. First, developments in literary criticism had produced a new kind of literary criticism, called the '**New Criticism**' in England and America and '**Formalism**' in Russia. New Criticism encouraged readers to look at works of literature not as 'messages' but as artefacts, 'verbal icons' to be valued for the skill with which they are constructed. They believed that literary criticism should concern itself primarily with how literary texts actually worked. As Terry Eagleton (1983) makes clear in his book *Literary Theory an Introduction*:

> The literary work was neither a vehicle for ideas, a reflection of social reality, nor the incarnation of some transcendental truth: it was a material fact, whose functioning could be analysed rather as one could examine a machine.   (p. 3)

This kind of criticism then was exclusively concerned with literary structure, prioritising form over content and focusing the attention upon language, perceiving the language of literature as an intensified and amplified form of everyday language which through its strange devices offers us a heightened awareness of the world:

> Literary discourse estranges or alienates ordinary speech, but in doing so, paradoxically, brings us into a fuller, more intimate possession of experience.   (p. 4)

Secondly, at the critical juncture of the inter-war period, a time of enormous social upheaval, those intellectuals who might previously have looked to religion for their moral instruction increasingly turned to literature. This period marks an important historical shift in the usage of the term 'morality'. From now on, morality is no longer to be understood as an explicit system of ethics, but rather a sensitive preoccupation with the whole quality of life itself.

These developments in literary theory, one formalistic, the other ethical and educative – might appear to be absolutely contraposed, but they founded an uneasy alliance in the theoretical developments of critics such as F. R. Leavis and others writing for the English journal *Scrutiny*. These critics believed that the uplifting and motivational power of literature was produced by its formal accomplishment. They insisted upon a rigorous analysis of the 'words on the page'. In this new climate of criticism, *Wuthering Heights* could also be positively reassessed; its extraordinarily complex structure was acknowledged and its enigmatic project became a sign of greatness.

 CHECK THE BOOK
C.P. Sanger, *The Structure of 'Wuthering Heights'* (1926) offers a contemporary example of how the approach to *Wuthering Heights* had changed in the 1920s.

Scrutiny insisted that how one evaluated literary texts was inevitably bound up with deeper judgements about the nature of history and society as a whole. However, *Wuthering Heights* still confounded its critics. The novel was too individual, too idiosyncratic. It was not, apparently, part of a literary heritage with clear ancestors and descendants. F R Leavis, the leading figure in the *Scrutiny* circle, could not allow that *Wuthering Heights* be admitted to his 'Great Tradition' of English literature because, he said: 'that astonishing work seems to me a kind of sport.'

Somewhat belatedly, Q. D. Leavis, F. R.'s wife and colleague, however, attempts to rescue the novel from such a dismissal with her essay 'A Fresh Approach to *Wuthering Heights*' (1969) in which she tries to establish what kind of a classic it might be.

Since then, arguments have ranged from whether Brontë's vision was social and historical or spiritual and **transcendent**, through whether or not the novel's mysteriousness arises from its profundity or its formal imperfections, to whether in fact it is possible, let alone desirable, to formulate a clear set of answers to the questions the novel presents. *Wuthering Heights* is a novel which is full of contradictions, a novel which defies stable readings, which is full of unresolved puzzles, unexplained dreams and unquiet ghosts.

Although profoundly shocking to some of its early readers, the novel nevertheless won some praise, as critics recognised its originality and sureness of touch. However, critical response has been unusually divided as to quite what constitutes the novel's success. Some critics have held that this is a timeless romance, a sweeping vision of high passion and the power of **romantic** love; others have maintained that the novel is deeply imbued with historical concerns, that it inevitably responds to its contemporary social, economic and political context. Frequently, its early critics complained about the novel's moral ambiguity, while nevertheless reluctant to deny its imaginative power. Shot through with passion the novel can be read as both love story and social commentary.

QUESTION

Is Heathcliff the hero of this novel? And what are the moral implications of such a reading?

Often acknowledged for being a subversive novel, *Wuthering Heights* is a novel in which ghosts and fantasies, dreams and visions subvert the natural or realist narrative. It is a novel in which heroes are unheroic and demons are beloved. It is a novel in which women are sometimes stronger than men; it is a novel which questions the foundations of marriage and the basis of marriage as women's complete subordination to men; it is a novel in which servants seem freer than their masters, for only Nelly Dean can pass unproblematically from the Heights to the Grange; it is a novel in which the boundaries between heaven and hell, between joy and salvation are reassessed and redrawn; and it is a novel in which traditional gender roles are confused, problematised and exploded, for, as Charlotte Brontë informs us:

> for an example of constancy and tenderness, remark that of Edgar Linton. (Some people will think these qualities do not shine so well incarnate in a man as they would do in a woman, but Ellis Bell could never be brought to comprehend this notion: nothing moved her more than any insinuation that the

faithfulness and clemency, the long-suffering and loving-kindness which are esteemed virtues in the daughters of Eve, become foibles in the sons of Adam.)
(Charlotte Brontë, editor's preface to *Wuthering Heights*, p. xxxv)

The world created by Brontë in this novel is equally conflicted in that it is one in which, as the feminist critics Sandra Gilbert and Susan Gubar suggest in *The Madwoman in the Attic*:

what seem to be the most unlikely of opposites coexist without, apparently, any consciousness on the author's part that there is anything unlikely in their coexistence.
(Sandra Gilbert and Susan Gubar, 1979, p. 259)

Criticisms of the novel that have focused on its 'confusion' and its 'incoherence' have tended to be moral judgements rather than formal. The Victorian judgement of the novel as 'confused' and 'wild' does not result so much from the complexities of its plot, or its structure, but from the fact that it fails to make its moral message clear. If we are to follow Matthew Arnold's notion that great literature is morally edifying, *Wuthering Heights* necessarily presents us with not inconsiderable difficulties, for this is a novel of profound moral ambivalence. The villains are not punished any more than the righteous, and indeed it is not often easy to distinguish between the two. There are no simple or straightforward answers to the questions raised by Brontë in *Wuthering Heights*: questions as to whether love or economic necessity must triumph; questions as to whether Heathcliff is the archetypal **romantic** hero, or an intrinsically evil character; questions about the ending of the novel, and how it causes us to reflect upon our initial assumptions. Indeed this novel raises far more questions than it answers, and as such has been identified as a profoundly disturbing novel by both early and contemporary critics.

The discrepancies between the various answers that have been suggested to these questions and the judgements made about the novel may well be perplexing and frustrating, but they also attest to the critical potency of this text. If words only meant one thing, and

CHECK THE BOOK
Julia Swindells' book, *Victorian Writing and Working Women* (1985) contextualizes some of the difficulties facing the Victorian woman writer.

meaning was stable and uncontestable then there would be no personal relationship with the text – why should I bother to read a novel if you could simply tell me what it says? If there were only one way of reading novels, one set of right answers to be elicited, then there would be no point in reading literature. It is the very incompatibility of **discourses** within literary texts that makes literature interesting and worthy of critical attention. It is the fact that the reading of literature gives rise to such fiercely contested arguments that makes us relish reading and want to return to the text with more information.

On one level this novel can be read as the supreme celebration of a love story, describing a love which defies authority, social convention, even death. Catherine and Heathcliff's love is famously deferred, never consummated and never translated into the pettiness of daily interactions. Theirs is a love which is idealised and magnified, and, in positing such a relationship, the novel both recognises and explicitly appeals to the desire for perfect love.

However, as Pauline Nester points out in her introduction to the 1995 Penguin Edition:

QUESTION

Is *Wuthering Heights* a love story, and what does it teach us about the nature of love?

> while the novel may seem to hold out the promise of such satisfaction on this level, in a more complex and more interesting way it actually investigates rather than exemplifies the romantic cliché of perfect love.
> (p. x)

Evidently the question of whether or not this story is the most consummate example of a love story is a very exercising one. Central to our understanding of the story is how we respond to the question of love. Is it love that characterises the relationship between Catherine and Heathcliff or is it, more perplexingly, just passion? If it is love, then theirs is a love which insists upon absolute identification with the beloved and which is ultimately fatal. If it is love then it is a love which requires the absolute sublimation of the self. If it is love, then it is a love so beyond the conventions of romantic love, positing at the end a necrophiliac obsession, that it is ultimately repellent.

The potency of the relationship between Catherine and Heathcliff brings to the novel its focus for examining the boundaries of identity. When Catherine declares to Nelly that she *is* Heathcliff, she offers a radical challenge to conventional notions of selfhood and individuality. Catherine's identification with Heathcliff in this passage utterly overwhelms her own discrete personal identity.

This throws into large relief the profound philosophical question of what happens to identity when individuality collides with love, in whatever form: sexual, romantic or religious.

Similarly, at a formal level, the repetitious doubling of names makes individual identity difficult to locate. Individual means indivisible, and Brontë's insistence upon merged or convergent identities destabilises fundamental notions about selfhood and responsibility. Evidently, there are moral as well as social implications in such postulations.

If *Wuthering Heights* suggests that to posit discrete identity is not as straightforward as we would normally imagine, it also takes an unconventional attitude towards gender identity. Clearly, in the sexual potency of his Byronic savagery, it is possible to read Heathcliff as the personification of stereotypical masculinity and Isabella, in her tragic romantic infatuation with him, as manifesting a version of femininity which provides its exact counterpart. However, in spite of such extremes, the novel offers an understanding of gender as demonstrably more equivocal than this: Catherine and Isabella may adopt certain versions of ladylike femininity, but they are versions that are ultimately fatal; Edgar is described as both fair and slight, but he is also referred to as 'the master', and he has the full weight of patriarchal privilege behind him; Heathcliff, by comparison, is an outcast, with no social position and no family until he contrives his own. Linton Heathcliff is depicted as relentlessly effeminate, more convincing as Edgar Linton's daughter than as Heathcliff's son, according to Joseph (p. 205). Equally, Catherine's energy, daring and mobility are more suggestive of conventional masculinity in the nineteenth century. In Romantic literature, reader expectation anticipates an antagonistic opposition of male sexual rivalry. In *Wuthering Heights* this

CONTEXT

Through the character of Joseph, Emily Brontë provides a phonetically accurate interpretation of the Yorkshire dialect. In her edition of Emily's novel, Charlotte Brontë modified the orthography to make it more intelligible to the reader.

antagonism would be between the legitimised patriarchal choice, Edgar Linton, and the dark, Byronic outsider, Heathcliff. However, in this novel any expectation of clear binary oppositions breaks down as the simple divide between true and false lover is negated by Edgar Linton's intransigence and Heathcliff's asexual indifference.

The novel both appeals to and subverts stereotypical constructions of sex roles by suggesting that strategies for survival are gender-related. So, for example, Heathcliff responds to oppression by plotting revenge, whereas Catherine turns to self-destruction. However, Brontë does not permit us simply to regard one response as inherently masculine and the other as feminine, because she makes clear that these strategies are determined as much by circumstance or opportunity as by gender – Isabella, for example, is inclined to violence, but lacks the means to inflict it:

> I surveyed the weapon inquisitively; a hideous notion struck me. How powerful I should be possessing such an instrument! I took it from his hand, and touched the blade. He looked astonished at the expression my face had assumed during a brief second. It was not horror, it was covetousness. He snatched the pistol back, jealously; shut the knife, and returned it to its concealment.
>
> (Vol. 1, Ch. 8, p. 138)

Similarly, Catherine boxes Edgar's ears for him on an early visit to Wuthering Heights, making Edgar 'afraid and ashamed' of her (Vol. 1, Ch. 3, p. 71).

This is a novel then that transgresses boundaries which Western culture has held particularly dear: social and sexual relations; the limits of life and death; personal responsibility; order and chaos; economic value and moral judgement. It is able to do so in part because of the importance of dreams in the novel.

QUESTION

Give an account of the role of dreams in this novel?

Dreams in this novel are both visionary and inexplicable. They are treated with respect and fear, and this is entirely appropriate for dreams offer the opportunity of presenting a world which operates in quite unpredictable and disturbing ways. Dreams also present us with ways of understanding the world which might otherwise be unthinkable. For Brontë, dreams offer a way of representing a reality which, according to the formal requirements of literary decorum expected of the nineteenth-century novel, is literally unwriteable. Small wonder then, that it received such puzzled and outraged reviews upon first publication:

> *Wuthering Heights* is a strange, inartistic story ... We know nothing in the whole range of our fictitious literature which presents such shocking pictures of the worst forms of humanity. (*Atlas*, January 1848)

Brontë is clear about her belief in the power of dreams to change lives, to affect reality directly:

> I've dreamt in my life dreams that have stayed with me ever after, and changed my ideas; they've gone through and through me, like wine through water, and altered the colour of my mind.
> (Vol. 1, Ch. 4, p. 79)

The centrality of dreams in this novel permits Brontë to tackle subjects in ways which she simply could not have attempted had she adhered to the limitations of what Julia Swindells (1985) has called the literary professionalism of the 'Gentleman's Club' in the nineteenth century.

The novel's violations and reinventions of identity, sexuality and taboo are as uncensored as in a dream: they are free from the restrictions of convention. The importance of dreams in this novel attests also to its pluralism. Dreams do not insist upon one story, they accommodate multiplicity. In dreams contradiction may well be disturbing, but it is not deleted. Indeed, it is part of the very structure of dreaming.

Wuthering Heights has also been noted for its generic ambiguity. Exactly what kind of novel is this 'rude and strange production'? If indeed it is a novel. It has been called an 'expanded fairytale' by Elliot Gose (1972, p. 233), a 'Romantic incest-story: Heathcliff as brother-lover;' by Q. D. Leavis, (in Rick Rylance, 1987, p. 145 see also pp. 24–30) and a 'psychological study' by numerous critics

CHECK THE BOOK
For a discussion of the literary relationships between *Wuthering Heights* and other literary texts, see Sandra Gilbert and Susan Gubar's *The Madwoman in the Attic* (1979), pp. 258–9.

both contemporary with the novel and those writing today. As Robert Kiely (1972) remarks:

> *Wuthering Heights* is like dream *and* like life *and* like history *and* like other works of literature precisely because Brontë rejects the exclusiveness of these categories. They continually inform and define one another.   (p. 236)

QUESTION

To what extent does the novel's 'generic uncertainty' contribute to its popularity?

And it is perhaps precisely this generic uncertainty which continues to beguile and intrigue so many readers. As the comforting pleasure of the familiar, provided by the text's realism, is challenged by the subversive power of the genres of fantasy and horror so the sheer enjoyment of the novel's romantic escapism is subtly counterpointed by the confidently combative stand it takes against convention. *Wuthering Heights* is a novel which causes us to reassess our conventional wisdom, to (re)consider the prejudices that we take for granted, to take delight in contradiction, for it is in contradiction that argument, theory and intellectual stimulation find their gratification.

There are many excellent editions of *Wuthering Heights*. The edition used in these Notes is the Penguin Classics Edition, 1995, edited with an introduction and notes by Pauline Nestor.

PART TWO

THE TEXT

NOTE ON THE TEXT

Wuthering Heights is Emily Brontë's only novel and it was published together with her sister Anne's novel, *Agnes Grey*, in December 1847 under the deliberately androgynous **pseudonyms** Ellis and Acton Bell. The Brontës' decision to use pseudonyms was one they had taken a year earlier with the publication of their poetry, *Poems by Currer, Ellis and Acton Bell*, because they wanted their poetry to receive due critical attention. As Charlotte explained: 'We had a vague impression that authoresses are liable to be looked on with prejudice' (Biographical Notice in *Wuthering Heights*, p. xxvii). The identity of the authors was revealed by Charlotte Brontë as she revised the text of the novel and added her preface to the second edition, published in 1850, two years after Emily Brontë's death. Most contemporary editions of the novel include Charlotte Brontë's prefaces. As Patsy Stoneman (1993) acknowledges:

> Charlotte Brontë's preface has had enormous influence on critics of later generations. Her notion of the involuntary creative process persisted from Matthew Arnold's memorial poem, 'Haworth Churchyard' (1855) to Peter Kominsky's 1992 film, *Emily Brontë's Wuthering Heights*, with its introductory sequence showing Emily 'inspired' by an old house on the moors.
>
> (p. 20)

The original readers of the 1850 edition, however, reacted less harshly to Charlotte Brontë's preface than to the Biographical Notice, which revealed for the first time the gender of the author. *Wuthering Heights* simultaneously challenged Victorian ideas about what was proper for literature and what was proper for a woman.

The pseudonym was not altogether unusual amongst Victorian authors. However, the adoption of pseudonyms by women writers

CONTEXT

It was not uncommon in Victorian times for authors to adopt a pseudonym – Dickens, for example, famously took Boz, and Thackeray called himself Titmarsh.

CHECK THE BOOK

Mrs Gaskell's, *The Life of Charlotte Brontë*, first published 1857 provides a useful account of the life of a woman writer in the nineteenth century.

has to be seen as part of a strategy against gender-specific prejudices and discrimination. Some of these gender prejudices are clearly articulated in the correspondence between Charlotte Brontë and Robert Southey, who argued: 'Literature cannot be the business of a woman's life, and it ought not to be.' Charlotte Brontë's reply which attempts to clarify the 'business of a woman's life, makes reference to the 'angel in the house' which has since been taken up by contemporary feminist critics Sandra Gilbert and Susan Gubar, most notably in their collection of essays *The Madwoman in the Attic: The Woman Writer and the Nineteenth-Century Literary Imagination* (1979).

Editions of the novel vary as to whether they retain the original two-volume structure, or whether they run the chapters on from one to thirty-four. These notes have assumed the structure of the original version.

SYNOPSIS

The story of *Wuthering Heights* is framed by two narrators, Lockwood, who commences and concludes the narrative, and Nelly Dean, who provides most of the narration.

The deferred passionate relationship between Catherine Earnshaw and Heathcliff is the single dominating feature of *Wuthering Heights*, driving the action of the novel forward in all its inexorable yet surprising directions. This is a dynastic novel, which plots the intertwined fortunes of three generations of the Earnshaws and the Lintons, fortunes which seem to repeat and revise the prime relationship between Catherine and Heathcliff. These repetitious revisions, the precise symmetry of the family trees and the mirrored relationships between the generations can themselves be read as taking up a contradictory position, serving both to establish continuity and succession, and equally to represent inertia and stagnation. These repetitious relationships are, as has been noted by Charles Percy Sanger in the Norton Critical Edition (eds Sale and Dunn, 1990) of *Wuthering Heights*: 'A remarkable piece of symmetry in a tempestuous book'. (p. 331) The function of such symmetry, he suggests, is to underline and confirm the eternal nature of enduring love.

The first three chapters detail Lockwood's relationship with his landlord, Heathcliff, and his experience of a sequence of visionary and inexplicable dreams in Heathcliff's home, Wuthering Heights. The narrative then passes to Nelly Dean, who takes us back in time to Heathcliff's arrival at the Heights as a child.

Catherine and Heathcliff grow up as siblings, after Heathcliff is introduced into the Earnshaw household by Catherine's father as a foundling and given the name of a dead son. Their relationship is one of intense identification. When their father dies, Catherine's brother Hindley returns to Wuthering Heights with a wife, Frances, and becomes the master of the house. Hindley's wish to sever the intimacy between Catherine and Heathcliff is given unexpected opportunity when Catherine spends five weeks at the neighbouring house, Thrushcross Grange, following a foot injury from their guard dog. Catherine returns to the Heights transformed into a lady, having made friends with the children of the Grange – Edgar and Isabella. While Catherine has been away, Hindley has systematically degraded Heathcliff, refusing him education, and insisting that he work as a labourer on the grounds. Hindley and Frances have a son, Hareton, and Frances dies shortly afterwards.

The events of the novel all resonate from the choice which Catherine makes to marry Edgar Linton rather than Heathcliff. How this choice is interpreted very much depends upon the critical stand one takes: it is possible to read it as economically inevitable, as profoundly immoral, as socially desirable, or as an act of perverse self-denial. These are not, of course, the only options available.

Following this choice, Heathcliff disappears for three years, and Catherine marries Edgar and moves to Thrushcross Grange. Her marriage to Edgar is described as affectionate, if subdued. In other words it conforms to the conventions of marriage in the nineteenth century. It is a marriage typified by a kind of quiet friendliness, and as such it is utterly at odds with what we have previously been given of Catherine's character.

CONTEXT

Wuthering Heights is believed to be based on a Yeoman house called High Sunderland which can be found near Law Hill, the school near Halifax where Emily taught in 1838.

Nelly Dean, the housekeeper moves with Catherine from the Heights. When Heathcliff returns he is quite transformed into an imposing and compelling figure of a man. He enraptures Catherine, and captivates Isabella, much to the annoyance of Edgar.

CONTEXT

Brontë's understanding of the intricacies of nineteenth-century property law is evident from the complex plot structure.

Heathcliff stays at Wuthering Heights, with his former enemy Hindley, with whom he gambles. In spite of Catherine's and Nelly Dean's warnings, Isabella falls in love with Heathcliff and Heathcliff perceives that she might well be his route to seeking revenge upon Edgar for depriving him of Catherine.

Edgar and Heathcliff argue violently, precipitating illness in Catherine. During the time that Catherine is ill, Heathcliff courts Isabella. Isabella and Heathcliff marry and Edgar disowns his sister.

For two months Edgar nurses Catherine, and there is no word from Isabella or Heathcliff. Then a letter from Isabella to Nelly Dean reveals that they are back at Wuthering Heights, and that the marriage is desperately unhappy. She begs Nelly to visit her. Edgar refuses to communicate with his sister, but Nelly goes to visit her and Heathcliff at the Heights. Heathcliff makes a passionate declaration of his love for Catherine, and an equally powerful vilification of Isabella. Nelly argues with him and berates him for his treatment of Isabella, but in the end relents and carries a letter from him to deliver to Catherine. This marks the end of the first volume.

The second volume commences with a visit from Heathcliff to Catherine. He perceives that her death is both imminent and inevitable. She dies that evening, giving birth to a daughter, Cathy, two months premature.

Isabella runs away from Heathcliff and her oppressive marriage. She departs for the South of England, where a few months later she gives birth to a son, Linton Heathcliff. At about this time Hindley dies leaving Heathcliff alone at the Heights with Hareton, whom Heathcliff treats as cavalierly as Hindley had treated him. When Isabella dies, Linton, now twelve and a sickly effeminate child, returns to Thrushcross Grange with Edgar. Heathcliff sends for him immediately and he is returned to Wuthering Heights to live with his father.

Cathy lives secluded but cherished at Thrushcross Grange, and her cousin's proximity is kept from her. On her sixteenth birthday, however, she chances to meet Heathcliff and Hareton on the moors and returns with them to Wuthering Heights where she is astonished to see Linton.

Heathcliff intends that Cathy and Linton should marry, for that way alone can he gain control of both houses, Wuthering Heights and Thrushcross Grange. Linton is sick and peevish, but Cathy's generous nature ensures that she feels a responsibility to making his life happier, a generosity which Heathcliff exploits fully.

Cathy is forbidden by Edgar to go back to the house, but contrives to write to Linton instead. Eventually though she gets the opportunity to pay him visits undetected by either Edgar or Nelly Dean.

Heathcliff's plan that the two cousins should marry is under time pressure, because Linton is so sick. Heathcliff's determination to revenge drives him to tyranny and eventually he forces a marriage between the two, since he is unable to manipulate events in any other way.

Edgar dies, Thrushcross Grange passes to Linton as the male progeny of Isabella, rather than to Cathy, as the female progeny of Edgar. But when Linton dies shortly afterwards, Heathcliff inherits what would otherwise have reverted to Cathy, since she is now his daughter-in-law. Thus cruelly dispossessed, Cathy lives a miserable existence at the Heights spurning any overtures of friendship from both Hareton and Zillah, the housekeeper. This brings us to the point at which Lockwood arrives as tenant of Thrushcross Grange, and introduces himself into the household.

The final three chapters of the second volume, mirroring the first three of the first, restore the narrative to Lockwood, who returns to the Heights a year later, to find that Heathcliff has died and Cathy and Hareton are enjoying a blissful courtship prior to their impending marriage.

> **CONTEXT**
>
> *Wuthering Heights* was originally published in two volumes. In its original edition it included a third volume which consisted of Anne Brontë's *Agnes Grey*.

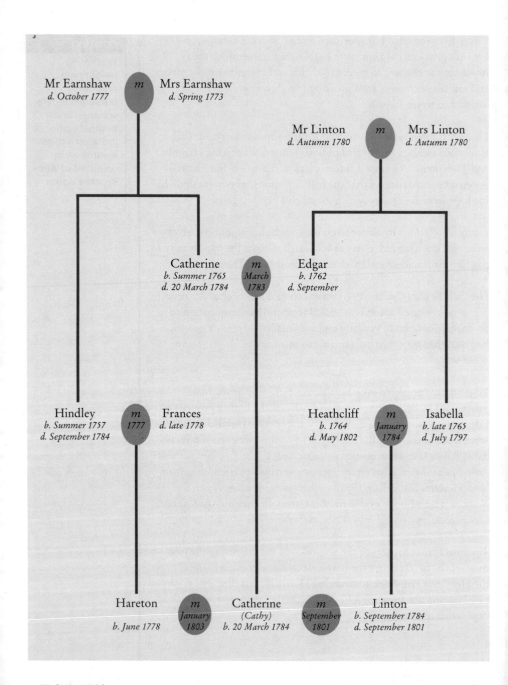

Mr Earnshaw
d. October 1777 **m** Mrs Earnshaw
d. Spring 1773

Mr Linton
d. Autumn 1780 **m** Mrs Linton
d. Autumn 1780

Catherine
b. Summer 1765
d. 20 March 1784 **m** *March 1783* Edgar
b. 1762
d. September

Hindley
b. Summer 1757
d. September 1784 **m** *1777* Frances
d. late 1778

Heathcliff
b. 1764
d. May 1802 **m** *January 1784* Isabella
b. late 1765
d. July 1797

Hareton
b. June 1778 **m** *January 1803* Catherine
(Cathy)
b. 20 March 1784 **m** *September 1801* Linton
b. September 1784
d. September 1801

DETAILED SUMMARIES

VOLUME ONE

CHAPTER 1

- Lockwood visiting Yorkshire pays his landlord, Heathcliff, a somewhat unwelcome visit in order to introduce himself.
- Introduction to Lockwood, Heathcliff, Heathcliff's servant Joseph and a female servant.
- Description of the property Wuthering Heights

GLOSSARY

penetralium the innermost parts or recesses of the building, most especially a temple. This use of a highly specialised Latinate term is indicative of Lockwood's education and sophistication

gnarl snarl

The chapter famously opens with the date 1801, suggesting both a new beginning and a diary entry. The narrator, Mr Lockwood, is visiting Yorkshire and is the new tenant of Thrushcross Grange. His landlord, who lives at Wuthering Heights, is Heathcliff, described by Lockwood as 'a dark-skinned gipsy in aspect, in dress and manners a gentleman' (p. 5). Lockwood is revealed as a rather self-satisfied and precious narrator, peculiarly insensitive to those he meets, and determined to see the world in conventional terms. We are offered a description of the threshold of Wuthering Heights, bearing the date 1500 and the name Hareton Earnshaw, but the history of the property is postponed as Lockwood is intimidated by the surliness of his landlord. In spite of a hostile welcome and an evident lack of desire on Heathcliff's part for the visit to be repeated, Lockwood nevertheless closes the chapter with a vow to return the following day.

COMMENTARY

As some critics, most notably C. P. Sanger, have noted, Brontë is at great pains to reflect chronological exactitude. Although the exact date is only mentioned three times, there are innumerable indications such as seasonal references and ages of characters which alert us to the complex time shifts in this novel. That chronological exactitude is of primary importance is established at the very beginning, since the first word of the novel is in fact the date, 1801. This date, suggestive as it is of a diary entry, grounds the fiction in

CONTEXT

'I never told my love' is a reference to Twelfth Night, Act II, Scene 4, lines 114–16, which establishes Lockwood as an educated narrator.

historical specificity. It sets up our expectations for the novel as a story set in reality, expectations which are then radically challenged as the narrative progresses, and is passed from Lockwood to Nelly Dean.

As Q. D. Leavis remarks in her essay 'A Fresh Approach to *Wuthering Heights*':

> The point about dating this novel as ending in 1801 (instead of its being contemporary with the Brontës' own lives) – and much trouble was taken to keep the dates, time-scheme and externals such as legal data accurate – is to fix its happenings at a time when the old rough farming culture based on a naturally patriarchal family life, was to be challenged, tamed and routed by social and cultural changes that were to produce the Victorian class consciousness and 'unnatural' idea of gentility.
>
> (Reprinted in Stoneman, 1993, p. 31)

Employing the use of the double narratives of Lockwood and Nelly (Nelly's narrative commences part way through the fourth chapter) was also a highly original technique, permitting Brontë to comment upon the nature of narratorial perspective.

GLOSSARY

Whet are ye for? What do you want?

i' t' fowld in the field

ut' laithe in the barn

flaysome fearful

discussed ate

un war and worse

a nowt a nothing, useless

agait afoot

nobbut strictly: nothing but; here: no-one but

shoo she

Wisht! Hush!

CHAPTER 2

- Lockwood repeats his visit to the Heights and meets Hareton and Catherine Heathcliff.

- Lockwood is obliged to spend the night as a guest at the Heights owing to hostile weather conditions.

Lockwood again visits Wuthering Heights the following afternoon, and arrives just as a snow shower begins. At first his way into the house is barred, and Joseph, hearing Lockwood's commotion, is most unhelpful. Lockwood meets, but is not introduced to, Hareton, who takes him in round the back. He also meets Cathy

Heathcliff, the 'missis' (p. 10), who is spectacularly surly. Hareton invites Lockwood to sit down. In stilted conversation with Cathy, Lockwood mistakes a heap of dead rabbits for a cushion full of cats, revealing him as an unreliable observer. Lockwood antagonises Hareton by trying to guess at the family and social relationships, and in the end Heathcliff reluctantly explains that both his wife and his son are dead, and that Cathy is his daughter-in-law.

Meanwhile the snow shower has turned into a blizzard, and Lockwood is finally obliged to stay the night. It is clear that he is most unwelcome, but Zillah, the housekeeper, takes pity on him and shows him to a bedroom.

COMMENTARY

This chapter clearly conveys the structural and social differences between Lockwood's expectations and the conventions he comes into contact with in Yorkshire. His desire to dine at five, for example, reflects a non-labouring lifestyle. Through the character of Joseph, Brontë provides a convincing rendition of Yorkshire dialect, which again serves to position Lockwood as an outsider, unable to comprehend the ordinary **discourse** of the region. Equipped with only his conventional notions of the world, Lockwood's pitiful misreading of the domestic situation stands as a warning against the adequacy of conventionality as a reliable reading of the world.

CHECK THE BOOK

Note another reference to Shakespeare on p. 17 – *King Lear*, Act II, Scene 4, lines 279–82.

CHAPTER 3

- Lockwood sleeps in a forbidden, secret room, and encounters the ghost of Catherine, much to Heathcliff's distress.

Zillah shows Lockwood to a room at the top of the house which, she confides, is both secret and forbidden. Mirroring the text within a text structure of the novel, this room contains within it a cleverly designed panelled structure which serves as both bed and little closet:

GLOSSARY

nut o'ered not over

lugs ears

laiking playing

scroop the spine of a book

pawsed his fit kicked his feet

laced thrashed

Grimalkin name of a cat, as for example the witches' cat Greymalkin, in *Macbeth*

> Having approached this structure, I looked inside, and perceived it to be a singular sort of old-fashioned couch, very conveniently designed to obviate the necessity for every member of the family having a room to himself. In fact, it formed a little closet, and the ledge of the window, which it enclosed, served as a table.   (p. 19)

QUESTION

Consider the importance of ghosts and spectres in this novel.

This interior room is home to a sparse mildewed library, which Lockwood peruses just before sleep. He also remarks upon the window-ledge which is covered with the name Catherine, in a number of manifestations: Catherine Earnshaw, Catherine Linton, Catherine Heathcliff. As he falls asleep, these versions of the name seem to Lockwood to swarm 'as vivid as spectres' (p. 20). He rouses himself to read through some of the books, and is surprised to discover the library is itself a **palimpsest**, every margin and space consumed with another writing, a text of Catherine's diary. Lockwood reads both the printed text: *Seventy Times Seven, and the First of the Seventy-first: a Pious Discourse delivered by the Rev. Jabes Branderham in the Chapel of Gimmerden Sough*, and the handwritten diary until he falls asleep.

While asleep he has two dreams:

First Dream: Lockwood is travelling with Joseph as his guide, when he discovers they are going not home but to see the Reverend Jabes Branderham preach. One of them, either Lockwood, or Joseph or the preacher, has committed the first of the seventy-first sins and is to be publicly denounced or excommunicated. Lockwood remonstrates with the preacher and reveals himself to be the sinner. He wakens from the dream to conclude that his sleep had been disturbed by the rapping of a branch against the window.

Second Dream: in this dream Lockwood is still aware of the branch tapping the window and resolves to stop it; however, when he reaches for the branch, his hand closes upon the icy fingers of a child. The child refuses to let go and begs to be allowed into the room. She identifies herself as Catherine Linton. In his terror Lockwood scrapes the hand backwards and forwards across the broken windowpane until the blood flows, the child releases her grip and Lockwood withdraws but cannot shut out her lament that

she has been waiting for twenty years to get back in the room.
Finally he cries out in fear and his cry brings Heathcliff to the scene.
Heathcliff rushes into the room and is dismayed to find Lockwood
installed.

Neither Lockwood nor Heathcliff can sleep for the rest of the night,
and Lockwood leaves Heathcliff in the room grieving for his 'heart's
darling' (p. 29), while he goes down to the kitchen, presently to be
joined by Joseph and Hareton.

Lockwood declines breakfast and makes his move back to
Thrushcross Grange at dawn. Heathcliff accompanies him back
across the moors and leaves him at the gate to the Grange,
whereupon Lockwood manages to double the distance to the house,
losing himself among the trees. He returns to Thrushcross Grange
full of self-pity feeling himself to be 'as feeble as a kitten' (p. 32), to
be attended by his housekeeper, Nelly Dean.

COMMENTARY

This is a chapter which has received much critical attention.
Containing Lockwood's two dreams, it clearly lends itself to a
psychoanalytical reading, a reading which treats the novel itself like
a dream, a fiction of the mind, which must be interpreted before its
meaning can be clearly apprehended. As Philip K. Wion points out
in his psychoanalytic reading of the novel, dreams and
hallucinations are forms of seeing in which the boundaries between
the self and the world are broken down, since in dreams, the
dreamer is often both an observer and a participant. The names
inscribed upon the windowsill might similarly be read as an
indicator of the conflicting elements of Catherine's identity.

**CHECK
THE BOOK**
*Fiction and
Repetition: Seven
English Novels,* by
J. Hillis Miller (1982)
offers a productive
and engaging
deconstructive
reading of this
chapter.

J. Hillis Miller's influential **deconstructive** reading of the chapter
discusses the **palimpsestic** nature of the texts, in which each text can
be seen as a commentary upon a previous one, in a movement which
extends inexorably back with no primary text ever reached. His
reading follows this trajectory: Catherine's diary is described by
Lockwood as a commentary, written in the margins of
Branderham's sermon. That sermon is itself a commentary upon
text of the New Testament in which Jesus enjoins his followers to

forgive seventy times seven. The first of the seventy-first is
therefore to be understood as the unpardonable sin. Jesus's
injunction is his interpretation of the nature of forgiveness, and
includes a reading of several phrases from the Old Testament.
Jesus's interpretation is characteristically accompanied by a **parable**.
A parable is an interpretation by means of a story which illustrates
that which is to be interpreted.

QUESTION

Consider the
importance of
repetition in
*Wuthering
Heights*.

Wuthering Heights can similarly be read as a **parable**, then, in that it
too is Lockwood's narration of a story which is adjacent to or in the
margins of the enigmatic events which he is trying to understand.
Miller's reading focuses attention on the role of margins in this
novel; he comments upon the difficulty of identifying the exact
beginning of the novel, prefaced as it is by so many introductions.
Lockwood's dreams can be seen as being exemplary of precisely this
difficulty of locating an exact beginning or precise meaning.

The description of Lockwood as a kitten serves to identify him as
similar to Edgar who is described as a cat in Chapter 8. Their
correspondences extend to their refined and fastidious natures, their
education and their social status.

Frank Kermode (1987) reads the repetitions of the names as both
indicative of the very isolated nature of the society, and also as an
encodement of the structure of the story:

> you see the point of the order of the scribbled names, as
> Lockwood gives them: *Catherine Earnshaw, Catherine
> Heathcliff, Catherine Linton*. Read from left to right they
> recapitulate the late Catherine Earnshaw's story; read from right
> to left, the story of her daughter, Catherine Linton. The names
> Catherine and Earnshaw begin and end the narrative ... this is an
> account of the movement of the book: away from Earnshaw and
> back, like the movement of the house itself. And all the
> movements must be through Heathcliff.   (p. 139)

A **structuralist** reading of the chapter would focus upon the
complex, interlocking structure of this text. What has been called its
'Chinese-box' structure by C. P. Sanger (1926). We have the

bedroom within the bedroom, the texts within the text which are themselves palimpsests, written over with Catherine's diary entries; the dreams, which contain sleepiness within sleeping, texts within texts again, and secrets within secrets.

CHAPTER 4

- Lockwood engages his housekeeper Nelly Dean to tell him the story of the inhabitants of Wuthering Heights, whereupon he and we learn something of Heathcliff's history and the family relationships that currently prevail.

The chapter commences with Lockwood finally admitting his need for human company and prevailing upon Nelly Dean to entertain him with local gossip. At this point Nelly Dean takes over the role of narrator. Primarily Lockwood is interested in the story of Wuthering Heights, and so we learn something of the early history of Catherine and Heathcliff and the various family relationships, both contemporary and historical. We learn that Cathy Heathcliff, condescendingly described by Lockwood as 'that pretty girl-widow' (p. 33) had married Heathcliff's son, and that her maiden name had been Linton. We learn that she is the last of the Lintons as Hareton is the last of the Earnshaws. Nelly hints that Heathcliff has cheated Hareton out of his rightful inheritance.

Nelly's story begins with the arrival of Heathcliff to the Heights as a child. Old Mr Earnshaw, Catherine's father returns to his family from a trip to Liverpool with the child as a 'gift from God' (p. 36). Other preliminary observations about Heathcliff remark him as a 'gipsy brat' (p. 37) and 'a dirty ragged black-haired child' (p. 36).

Earnshaw's children, Catherine and Hindley immediately dislike the newcomer because the presents which their father had promised them, a fiddle for Hindley and a whip for Catherine, had been either crushed or lost on the way home. Mrs Earnshaw too is appalled at the idea of having another child to feed and clothe. But Mr

Earnshaw is adamant and the 'cuckoo' (p. 35) remains as a family member and is christened Heathcliff after a son who had died in childhood. The name Heathcliff serves the child as both Christian and surname from that point on. From the very outset then, Heathcliff occupies a conflictual and contradictory position in the household, and in the story. He is 'a gift of God' (p. 36), a ghostly substitute for a dead elder son, and he is 'a wicked boy' (p. 62) 'possessed of something diabolical' (p. 74) He is also quite beyond the formal societal constraints of the family and the Church, having but one name that serves him for both purposes.

QUESTION

Consider the ways in whcih Heathcliff, both orphan and imposter, works against the coherent order of the novel.

Eventually Heathcliff and Catherine become firm friends, but his presence in the household remains divisive, as Hindley continues to hate him and Mr Earnshaw makes him his favourite. Two years later Mrs Earnshaw dies and the children all fall sick with the measles. This endears Heathcliff to Nelly Dean as he is least complaining, unlike Hindley and Catherine. Heathcliff's stoicism and patience which here are the qualities that endear him to Nelly, are precisely the qualities that he draws on later to such devastation. The chapter closes with the incident of the two colts. Heathcliff takes the best and, when his falls lame, takes Hindley's. Hindley's behaviour towards Heathcliff is brutish and violent. Heathcliff, once he gets his way is self-contained and apparently unvindictive, though tantalisingly Nelly confides that in this assessment she was 'deceived, completely' (p. 40). Read in conjunction with the qualities he shows in illness Heathcliff's attitude here can be seen as revealing of his unwavering ambition and determination to achieve his heart's desire. He sees no point in wasting emotional energy, and he is oblivious to the emotional life of others.

COMMENTARY

The most significant aspect of this chapter is the change of narrator from Lockwood, whom we have come to perceive as unreliable, to Nelly Dean who has the advantage of having lived with the main protagonists and who is thus able to gloss their characters for Lockwood. This doubling of narrator acts, as J. Hillis Miller reminds us, as a caution to the overconfident reader, for it immediately unsettles our certainty that the narrator's voice is neutral or trustworthy. This device of an external masculine narrative framing and legitimating an internal feminine narrative was also used by Anne Brontë in *The Tenant of Wildfell Hall*, and can be seen in relation to Brontë's use of the suggestively masculine **pseudonym** to legitimate her novel.

Notwithstanding the ultimate success of this novel, Brontë was evidently alive to the potential for being overlooked or dismissed as a female author, and indeed Charlotte Brontë openly acknowledges their motives for choosing gender-neutral pseudonyms: '...we did not like to declare ourselves women, because ...we had a vague impression that authoresses are liable to be looked on with prejudice' (p. xxvii).

It is noteworthy that when Nelly Dean takes up the narration we are presented with a narrative whose subject and interest consist entirely of domestic action and adventure. The structure of power is an important theme for Brontë, and she treats it in a highly nuanced and complex way, revealing its contradictory yet never confused relationships. While she is clearly aware of and understands the impact of property laws upon women's wealth and influence, Brontë nevertheless cautions us against underestimating the domestic power that women are sometimes able to operate. In the final analysis it is her female characters who have the upper hand: Cathy, bathed in glowing moonlight and the warmth from the fire is teaching a willingly submissive Hareton his letters; similarly Nelly is able to silence the lugubrious Joseph, and expertly manages the financial affairs of the properties.

QUESTION

Consider the theme of power in this novel with reference to two of the following: Nelly Dean, Catherine Earnshaw or Isabella Linton.

Brontë's understanding of power is sophisticated. She clearly believes that power operates in many different ways, and is available to serve different ends. She is unflinching in her understanding of its social implications, in which power might be seen in terms of its patterns of domination: the despotism of the strong over the weak, the inequalities between men and women, and between rich and poor.

She is equally clear about the power of writing: the power that attaches to what has been called the 'production of meaning'; the power of language to influence our emotions and our attitudes; the manipulative potential of communication.

The relationship between these different kinds of power is elegantly exemplified in the relationship between the two narrators. Lockwood, although he is woefully incapable of reading the discourse of his new environment and utterly incompetent at understanding the writing on the sill, is nevertheless able as a man, and as Heathcliff's tenant, to prevail upon Nelly Dean to sit and tell him stories way beyond her working hours. Nelly, on the other hand, reader of all the books in the library and recipient of important letters, controls a great deal of the action of the novel through her choices about what to do with such privileged information.

The arrival of Heathcliff at the Heights has been the focus of much critical attention. In *The Madwoman in the Attic: The Woman Writer and the Nineteenth-Century Literary Imagination*, Sandra Gilbert and Susan Gubar (1979) read this arrival in terms of its gender implications, paying attention to the whip as a symbol of masculinity, which Catherine has requested and which is lost only to be replaced by Heathcliff. In *Myths of Power: A Marxist Study of the Brontës*, a **Marxist** reading of the novel, Terry Eagleton (1992) sees Heathcliff's presence at the Heights as both radical and random. Because Heathcliff's origins are so obscure, and because his family relationships place him outside the conventional social structure of the family, he is available to be loved or hated for himself. His lack of social status or clear social role, coupled with Mr Earnshaw's favouritism, destabilises any certainty about inheritance and genealogy, causing Hindley to feel, rightly, threatened, and Catherine, equally rightly, strengthened.

GLOSSARY
made the living answer supplemented his income
wick lively
frame hurry

CHAPTER 5

• Nelly Dean recounts how the family relationships develop as Mr Earnshaw's health fails. First sustained description of Catherine.

As Mr Earnshaw's health begins to fail his partiality towards Heathcliff becomes even more pronounced. Hindley continues to scorn Heathcliff, which enrages his enfeebled father. The family curate, who has supplemented his income by teaching the Earnshaw children advises that Hindley be sent to college, to which Earnshaw agrees, though considers his eldest son unlikely to succeed at anything.

The first description of Catherine shows her as beautiful, lively and wayward, but with a good heart: 'A wild, wick slip she was – but she had the bonniest eye, and the sweetest smile, and the lightest foot in the parish; and after all, I believe she meant no harm' (p. 42). Mr Earnshaw dies quietly one October evening. Both Catherine and Heathcliff are utterly distraught, and comfort one another.

COMMENTARY

The focus of this chapter is Catherine's relationships with her father and Heathcliff of whom, Nelly avers, Catherine is much too fond. However, the description of Catherine as deliberately infuriating and rebellious, and indeed of Heathcliff as some sort of devilish progeny is counterbalanced by their response to her father's death, which Nelly describes as both anguished and innocent. Contradiction is seen to be an integral part of the way in which people relate to each other. It is this acknowledgement of internal contradiction that has given rise to the criticisms of the moral ambivalence of this novel. It is also worthy of note that at this early point in the novel Brontë is already pitting an unmediated spiritual belief against the stern religious dogma of Joseph.

The passage has been read as an example of the **romantic** theme of the child in conflict with society. If we are to accept such a reading then it is noteworthy that Brontë permits Catherine the last word: 'Why cannot you always be a good man, father?' (p. 43).

 CHECK THE BOOK
Emily Brontë often refers to the comfort to be gained from the idea of an afterlife in Heaven. See for example, a Gondal poem dated 1841, in Emily Brontë, *The Complete Poems* (p. 137).

GLOSSARY

foreigners strangers

lascar East-Indian
seaman

negus hot toddy made
of wine and water

CHAPTER 6

- Following the death of his father, Hindley returns as the master of the Heights, with a wife, Frances.

- He endeavours to make Heathcliff's life a misery, but Catherine and Heathcliff remain inseparable and wild.

- Catherine is hurt on one of their escapades and remains at the neighbouring house, Thrushcross Grange, until she is considered well enough to return to the Heights.

Hindley comes home for the funeral accompanied by a wife, Frances, who is described as poor, ill and silly. As the new master of the Heights, Hindley finds vent for all his old hatred of Heathcliff. He denies him an education, insists that he should labour out of doors and makes him live with the servants. None of this at all detracts from Catherine and Heathcliff's bond, and they are united in their naughtiness 'and the after punishment grew a mere thing to laugh at' (p. 46). One night when they cannot be found Hindley instructs that the doors be bolted against them. When Heathcliff returns alone, it emerges that Catherine has remained at Thrushcross Grange where they have been peeping in at the Lintons, who live there. There follows the first introduction to Edgar Linton and his sister Isabella, as 'petted things' (p. 48). Once observed, they are set upon by the guard dogs and Catherine is caught by the ankle and savaged, thus she is unable to return to the Heights with Heathcliff. The next day Mr Linton remonstrates with Hindley for being unable to run his household properly, Heathcliff is forbidden to talk to Catherine, and Frances undertakes to keep Catherine in due restraint.

CONTEXT

This depiction of
domestic violence
is entirely in
conflict with the
conventional
Victorian notion of
the home as the
ideal refuge from
the harshness of
the outside world.

COMMENTARY

The chronology of this chapter takes us back to the point in time of Catherine's diaries, read by Lockwood in Chapter 3.

Critical attention to this chapter has often focused upon the structural differences between Thrushcross Grange and Wuthering Heights. The splendid, cultivated and civilised atmosphere at the

Grange is compared with the rough indiscipline of the Heights. Most famously David Cecil has argued that the differences between the Heights and the Grange can be thought of as corresponding to a metaphysical opposition between storm and calm. And yet, as Gilbert and Gubar (1979) point out the violence which one might naturally associate with the Heights is no less present at the Grange. They argue that Catherine, for example, does not so much willingly enter the world of Thrushcross Grange, as be seized by it. Indeed, as Terry Eagleton (1992) points out, the more property one has, the more ferociously one needs to protect it. In their reading of the novel in Chapter 8 of *The Madwoman in the Attic*, the feminist critics Sandra Gilbert and Susan Gubar see *Wuthering Heights* as a 'Bible of Hell' in that it is a novel which privileges the natural over the cultural, the freedom of anarchy over domesticated repression. The domain of Wuthering Heights is certainly infernal judged by conventional standards. Indeed we are encouraged to read it as hellish by Lockwood in Chapter 2 with his remarks upon the 'dismal spiritual atmosphere' (p. 14) and Heathcliff's 'almost diabolical' (p. 13) smile. But it can also be read as representing another challenge to convention in as much as it is an ungovernable social space. As such it is a space in which both Catherine and Heathcliff can exercise power, a facility which would have been refused to both of them in the nineteenth century, she being female and he being illegitimate.

As Ruth Robbins clarifies in *Literary Feminisms* (2000):

> Thrushcross Grange, across the moor, home of the Linton family, represents the standards of patriarchal culture which will be triumphant at the end of the story, but which the novel itself, through its sympathies for Cathy and Heathcliff, implicitly attacks.   (p. 92)

Captured, in fairytale manner, by the 'civilised' world of Thrushcross Grange, Catherine yields to what she understands to be her destiny, even as she recognises this as an act of bad faith; later, anguished and despairing she resists it and finds her only way out of it by death. Literally she 'catches her death' by throwing open the window in Chapter 12. This act of opening the window can be read as rupturing the fortifications of the civilised life to let in the fresh

> **CONTEXT**
>
> Catherine's courage is reminiscent of Emily Brontë's own fearlessness with dogs. In one incident, Emily used a red hot iron to cauterise a wound she sustained from a ferocious dog.

air of the natural, an act of such symbolic violence it can only result in death.

This chapter gives the child Heathcliff his first major speech, and it is worth noting how his language differs from that of the other characters. He is expressive and emotional, and this encourages us to identify very profoundly with his unmediated, unguarded response. His speech is more literary than Ellen's and less artificial than Lockwood's. He tends to speak in extreme and vibrant terms: expressing his scorn for Edgar Linton's cowardice and plaintive gentility, he says:

> I'd not exchange, for a thousand lives, my condition here, for Edgar Linton's at Thrushcross Grange – not if I might have the privilege of flinging Joseph off the highest gable, and painting the house-front with Hindley's blood! (p. 48)

Note that in aligning ourselves with Heathcliff as the vital and wronged party here we are already accepting and endorsing the violence that is to characterise his behaviour as the novel progresses. Heathcliff's threat to paint the house with Hindley's blood and fling Joseph off the gable top is an empty one at this point, but it nevertheless presages what is to come. It can also be read as representing a real desire to topple conventional religious authority in favour of a more 'natural' spirituality and to sever the authority of Hindley's bloodline, making Wuthering Heights his own.

Heathcliff admires the comparative luxury of the Grange and acknowledges its beauty. He even compares it to a kind of heaven, but he remains entirely devoted to the freedom of his life with Catherine, and cannot comprehend the selfishness of the spoiled children: 'When would you catch me wishing to have what Catherine wanted?' (p. 48)

This question is rhetorical. What Heathcliff cannot imagine is quarrelling with Catherine over something she wants, since their needs and desires are exactly matched. What appals him are the opposing, individual, selfish needs of the Linton children.

QUESTION

Consider Brontë's treatment of conventional authority in this novel with reference to two of the following: religion, marriage, education, law or domesticity.

The image of the two civilised children inside the beautiful room, and the two wild children outside, both boy and girl of similar ages, can be read as figuring the glass of the window as a kind of mirror. However, this is a mirror which reflects opposition, desire, and otherness. It has thus offered itself as rich territory for both **structuralist** and **psychoanalytic** readings.

CHAPTER 7

GLOSSARY
cant lively

- Catherine returns from her five-week stay at Thrushcross Grange, transformed into a lady.
- Heathcliff has been systematically further debased by Hindley during this time.
- The end of this chapter reminds us that this is a story being related to Lockwood by Nelly Dean.

Catherine stays at Thrushcross Grange for five weeks until she is deemed healthy, both in body and manners. She returns to the Heights a very 'dignified person' (p. 52) dressed in fine clothes and quite transformed from the person she had been. Heathcliff, by contrast, is forbiddingly unkempt, but Catherine's love of him is undiminished and she embraces him immediately. The Linton children have been invited over the next day in order to thank them for tending Catherine. Heathcliff begs Nelly to make him decent. Hindley and Edgar Linton combine to discredit and humiliate Heathcliff, who retaliates violently. Heathcliff is dismissed and Catherine apparently unfeelingly continues to have tea with her new friends. Eventually she creeps away from the tea party to be with Heathcliff, and Heathcliff plots his revenge on Hindley.

Finally Nelly Dean interrupts her narrative to focus upon Lockwood, who requires her to continue her story even though the hour is late. Lockwood comments on the class and type of people he has encountered in the region, and Nelly recalls to us his hasty

CHECK THE BOOK

Michael Macovski's essay 'Voicing a Silent History: 'Wuthering Heights' as Dialogic Text' (1987) reprinted in Patsy Stoneman (1993) offers an interesting reading of the novel as a series of stories.

judgements and his condescension by remarking that he 'could not open a book in this library that [she had] not looked into' (p. 62). Lockwood's failure to read Nelly Dean in any terms other than the conventions of class is further reinforced by his insensitivity to Nelly's hours of sleep and work. She characteristically deflates his pompous exposition upon the type of people native to the region by drawing attention to both her level of formal education and the lessons learned from the exacting discipline of her life. Brontë emphasises the potency of female **discourse** with Nelly's account here. Lockwood's inability to contemplate the broader picture is perceived by both Nelly and the reader to be a failure of intellect as much as of experience.

COMMENTARY

Once again critical attention might be paid to the boundaries and barriers in this chapter. Just as the window separated the Wuthering Heights' children from the Lintons in the last chapter, once again a material object separates Catherine from Heathcliff in this one. The fine dress she wears to return to the Heights represents a very real boundary between the old friends: it must be sacrificed (smudged, crumpled) if the two of them are to be as close as they were before. It is simultaneously valuable for economic reasons (its cost), for social ones (the respect it affords Catherine), and because of its artificial beauty. These same categories will consistently come between Cathy and Heathcliff; he is right to recognise the dress and what it represents as a threat to his happiness. The dress thus signifies the artifice of civilisation which Catherine must put on and which will alienate her from Heathcliff with devastating consequences.

The bed to which Heathcliff retires hurt is precisely the bed which had housed Lockwood's disturbing dreams in the third chapter. Here too, its panels and windows operate to form a series of boundaries behind which secrets can be concealed.

CHAPTER 8

- Hindley's son Hareton is born.
- Frances Earnshaw dies of consumption and Hindley declines even further into recklessness.
- The relationship between Catherine and Edgar is developed and the tension between Edgar and Heathcliff is intensified.

In June 1778 Hareton Earnshaw is born as the son to Hindley and Frances. Not long afterwards Frances dies of consumption and Nelly Dean is bidden to Wuthering Heights to act as nursemaid to the baby. Hindley goes into a decline at the death of his wife and relinquishes himself to drinking and dissolute behaviour. Catherine is now fifteen years old and Edgar Linton has taken to calling on her. Nelly's account of Edgar is that he 'wanted spirit in general' (p. 66). Nelly details Catherine's conflicting alliances with both Heathcliff and Edgar. Catherine's reluctance for them to meet stems from the feeling that their differences only highlight her own internal conflicts. Catherine and Heathcliff quarrel as she chooses to spend more time with the Lintons than with him, and when Edgar comes to call Catherine reacts badly to Nelly's presence in the room, pinching her and slapping her face, which she then promptly lies about. Edgar is shocked at her behaviour and attempts to intervene, earning himself a box on the ears. Edgar makes to leave, but in spite of himself cannot bear to part with her and eventually only leaves when Hindley returns home drunk.

CONTEXT
Hindley's wife exhibits the symptoms of tuberculosis or consumption, the disease which was to claim the lives of both Emily and Anne Brontë within six months of each other in 1848–9.

COMMENTARY

This chapter first explicitly details the central conflict of the novel, the choice that Catherine has to make between Heathcliff and Edgar Linton. The choice is pivotal to all the events in the novel, and has been variously seen as a choice between passion and social status, authenticity and bad faith, sex and sublimation, risk and security, nature and culture, spirituality and economics. However it is framed, the choice is almost always seen as being between two incompatible ways of life.

Dorothy Van Ghent in her **formalist** analysis of the novel *The English Novel: Form and Function* (1961) focuses her attention upon the significance of the numerous windows and doors in this novel, arguing that such formal boundaries represent the tension between these two conflicting realities. She draws attention to the ways in which different characters aim to cross these physical boundaries and unite the two kinds of reality, and argues that although for Catherine Earnshaw the attempt results in her death, suggesting that the choice is really about irreconcilable realities, by the end of the novel, Catherine Heathcliff does succeed in achieving the domestic romance.

QUESTION

'The self exists both subjectively and objectively, but never integrally'. Consider with reference to Cathy's characterisation in this chapter.

Van Ghent's thesis has been immensely influential, and has been included in many subsequent readings, and a dedicated trawl for consistent symbols and images is now a standard method of reading a text like *Wuthering Heights*. Influencing not only literary criticism but also film versions and a recent video study-guide by 'Literary Images', which:

> Filmed on location in the village of Haworth and on the Yorkshire moors ...looks closely at the major themes and images of the novel. We find, for instance, the elements of earth, air, fire and water, which have their origin in the landscape which Emily knew and loved.

> Here too are the 'barrier' images of windows, doors and gates ... the landscape ... is still there ... and this video has captured it in all its detail – 'the elemental rocks beneath' ... Cathy's rustling 'heaven', the moths on the heather and the harebells of the last paragraph   (Quoted in Stoneman, 1993, p. 51)

CHAPTER 9

- Catherine makes her choice between Edgar and Heathcliff and chooses Edgar.
- Heathcliff disappears.

- Catherine catches a fever and goes once more to recuperate at the Grange.
- Three years later, when Edgar is master of the Grange, he marries Catherine.
- Nelly reluctantly leaves Hareton and goes with Catherine to the Grange.

Heathcliff and Hindley's relationship deteriorates even further. Hindley is abusive and violent to everyone, threatens Nelly with a carving knife and shows no affection for his infant son. Hareton falls from Hindley's arms over the stairwell only to be caught by Heathcliff who cannot believe that he has done Hindley a favour. After this Heathcliff retires to the dark end of the kitchen where he remains unobserved and silent. Catherine comes in and confesses to Nelly that Edgar has asked her to marry him. She has already given Edgar her answer, but nevertheless wishes Nelly to say what the answer should have been. There follows an exposition on the nature of love during which Catherine shows her feelings for Edgar to be based upon his looks, his disposition and his wealth. She believes that she has no more business to marry him than she has a right to heaven. She announces that it would degrade her to marry Heathcliff, whereupon Heathcliff leaves the kitchen and the household. After his departure, which goes unobserved by Catherine, she goes on to say how she will never forsake Heathcliff, and the chapter contains the famous line: 'Nelly, I *am* Heathcliff' (p. 82).

Nelly reveals to Catherine that Heathcliff has overheard part of what she had said and Catherine distressed at the possible consequences rushes out into the night to try and find him. She sits the whole night outside, catches a chill and becomes dangerously ill with a fever. Mrs Linton insists that she return to Thrushcross Grange to convalesce, but she and her husband then both catch the fever and die, leaving Edgar as the master of the Grange. Once again Catherine returns to the Heights haughtier than she left.

Three years later, during which time Heathcliff has never returned, Catherine marries Edgar and Nelly is bidden to accompany her

CONTEXT

The ballad that Nelly sings to Hareton expresses the widely held belief in folklore and folksong, that a prematurely dead mother cannot rest in the grave but will return to suckle her baby or help her child when it is in need. It is thus prescient of what is to come.

CHECK THE BOOK

Heather Glen gives a good, non-technical description of this process in the 'Critical Commentary' in her edition of *Wuthering Heights* (1988, pp. 360–1).

against her will to Thrushcross Grange, leaving Hareton to the negligent and cruel inclinations of his father, alone in Wuthering Heights. The final paragraph of the chapter returns the narrative to Lockwood, who observes the housekeeper note the time and they repair to their beds.

COMMENTARY

The central dichotomy of the novel is revealed here as being a choice about love and the nature of love. Catherine expounds her thoughts on love through a dream she has had about being unfit to enter heaven. **Psychoanalytic** critics have focused their attention on the dreams in this novel and the ways in which desire is sublimated into other, destructive, channels. Other critics such as **Marxist** and **feminist** critics have read this decision in terms of its political ramifications.

For many readers, the fascination and enduring appeal of *Wuthering Heights* lies in its evocation of romantic love, the state of being utterly absorbed in another person which Lacanian psychoanalysis identifies as a powerful nostalgic re-enactment of the pre-linguistic symbiosis of mother and child. The psychologist Jacques Lacan identifies an important phase of human development as being what he calls the 'mirror phase' of infancy, in which the self is defined not through language but through the reflecting gaze of somebody else (usually the mother) who is 'more myself than I am'. Psychoanalytic readings have evidently made much of his theories. Yet the novel is, necessarily, bound in words; it can only gesture towards this pre-linguistic state in what is, strictly speaking, linguistic non-sense: 'I *am* Heathcliff'.

Catherine's declaration of love for Heathcliff comes at precisely the moment that she has chosen to marry Edgar, and at the point at which Heathcliff disappears from their lives. It is therefore possible to read this as indicative of the ways in which the consummation of passion is endlessly deferred in favour of social convention and restraint. Catherine's immoderate love for Heathcliff, which causes her to stay outdoors until she catches the chill which proves deadly to Mr and Mrs Linton, can thus be read as a love which is fatally inadmissible to the civilised life. Catherine's avowal that anyone who tried to keep her and Heathcliff separate would 'meet the fate of Milo' (p. 81) can be read as indicative of her own unacknowledged perception of herself as trapped. Such a reading can be corroborated when Heathcliff declares at the end of the first volume 'And that insipid, paltry creature attending her from *duty* and *humanity*! From *pity* and *charity*! He might as well plant an oak in a flower pot and expect it to thrive, as imagine he can restore her to vigour in the soil of his shallow cares!' (p. 151).

CHAPTER 10

- Catherine Earnshaw now married to Edgar Linton, lives in relative luxury and peace with Edgar and his sister Isabella.
- Heathcliff returns to Catherine's immense jubilation.
- Heathcliff reveals that he is staying with Hindley at the Heights.
- Isabella develops an intense fascination for Heathcliff who, while he does not return the sentiment, nevertheless sees that he might use her attraction for him as a way to revenge himself upon Edgar.

The chapter opens with Lockwood feeling most sorry for himself after four weeks of illness and a visit from Heathcliff. Lockwood calls for Nelly Dean to resume her narrative. Nelly's story recommences with the marriage of Edgar and Catherine. As Catherine Linton, Catherine's life is one of gentle cultivation, largely because she is endlessly indulged by both Edgar and Isabella. Life is simple and happy until the return of Heathcliff.

Heathcliff's return is the source of fervent joy for Catherine. Nelly details the transformation of Heathcliff into a tall, intelligent man in whom passion is observable but subdued. It emerges that Heathcliff is staying with Hindley Earnshaw at Wuthering Heights, which causes Nelly to be suspicious.

Visits between Heathcliff and Catherine become more frequent and Isabella develops an intense fascination for Heathcliff which irritates

Edgar and worries Catherine. Catherine divulges Isabella's attraction to Heathcliff and sows the seed of the idea for revenge into Heathcliff's mind. Heathcliff hints that he will use Isabella's devotion to win his revenge over Edgar.

COMMENTARY

The return of Heathcliff to the text restores to it some of its sinister energy. It also seems to enliven Catherine and Isabella, taking them out of the atmosphere of the house and onto the moors or up to the Heights. Here, however, Heathcliff has learned to dissemble in order to obtain his desires, and we are reminded both of his first visit to Thrushcross Grange, when he despised its inhabitants for their pettiness and selfishness and of his self-control in the appropriation of Hindley's horse (Vol. 1, Ch. 4).

Catherine's betrayal of Isabella's confidence to Heathcliff is actually a misrepresentation of what Isabella has declared, for she tells him 'Isabella swears that the love Edgar has for me is nothing to that she entertains for you' (p. 104) whereas Isabella in fact says 'I love him more than you ever loved Edgar' (p. 101). And this misrepresentation too is available for **psychoanalytic** critical analysis.

GLOSSARY

barn child

sandpillar milestone

CHAPTER 11

- Nelly returns on a whim to the Heights and is appalled to see how it has deteriorated.
- Heathcliff calls at the Grange and makes overtures to Isabella, displeasing both Catherine and Edgar.
- Fierce arguments between Catherine, Edgar and Heathcliff induce Catherine to retire to her bed.

Reminiscence marks the opening of this chapter as Nelly Dean fondly remembers both her own childhood with Hindley and her affection for Hareton. Ten months have passed since she left the Heights and now she returns there on a whim to observe it and its inhabitants once more..Hareton, though barely more than five, curses her. Heathcliff, it emerges, has set son against father and is breeding insurrection in the already unhappy household. When Heathcliff appears, Nelly returns swiftly to the Grange.

Heathcliff's next visit to the Grange sees him capitalise upon Isabella's affection. Catherine requests him to desist from his attentions to Isabella if he wishes to remain welcome, and he and Catherine argue. Heathcliff tells Catherine that she has behaved abominably to him, and that he is set on revenge against the Lintons. Edgar, hearing of Catherine's distress, resolves to throw Heathcliff out. They come to blows and Catherine retires to her bed claiming herself to be 'in danger of being seriously ill' (p. 115). Forced to choose between Edgar and Heathcliff, she threatens to break their hearts by breaking her own. Nelly treats Catherine's outburst as histrionics and fails to take her threatened illness seriously. Catherine departs to her room and refuses any nourishment for the next two days. Edgar retires to the library and tries to dissuade Isabella from her infatuation with Heathcliff, claiming that if she continues in it, then he will disown her.

COMMENTARY

Once again the central choice of the novel takes up the majority of this chapter. Critical attention has focused upon the role of illness as a sign for femininity in the nineteenth century. Emily Brontë can be seen to be writing about illness as a female strategy here: rather than indicating simply weakness, illness becomes a way of for Catherine to influence the actions of both Edgar and Heathcliff.

> **CONTEXT**
>
> The **romantic** view is that illness exacerbates consciousness, and this too affords Catherine, Isabella and later Cathy some influence. Evidently this is a risky, ultimately fatal, strategy for both Catherine and Isabella.

CHAPTER 12

- Catherine is truly ill.
- Isabella leaves secretly to marry Heathcliff.
- Edgar disowns Isabella.

GLOSSARY

caps outshines

pigeon feathers
referral to a
superstition that the
soul of a dying person
could not leave the
body if the mattress or
pillow were stuffed
with pigeon feathers

elf-bolts flint
arrowheads

Isabella mopes; Edgar reads; Catherine starves herself. After three days Catherine is convinced she is dying, and is incredulous at Edgar's apparent unconcern. Edgar is so far ignorant of Catherine's condition, since Nelly Dean still believes Catherine's illness to be manufactured in order to manipulate. Now, however, Nelly recalls Catherine's earlier illness and begins to be alarmed for her as Catherine starts to hallucinate. Catherine is delirious and feverish and Edgar, upon entering her room, is horrified at her condition. He blames Nelly for her deterioration, and Nelly goes into the garden to find Isabella's favourite dog hanging from a tree, almost dead. Nelly summons the doctor to attend to Catherine, and the doctor informs her that Isabella and Heathcliff have been having secret nightly trysts and intend to elope. Nelly returns to the Grange to find that Isabella has already left with Heathcliff, but does not tell Edgar because he is so worried about Catherine. The next day Edgar learns of Isabella's departure and disowns her.

COMMENTARY

Critical attention might well be devoted to the role of Nelly Dean in this chapter, since she is the person who controls all the key critical information: Catherine's illness and Isabella's departure.

Nelly's assumption that Catherine's illness is invented by her in order to manipulate gives credence to the reading that women in the nineteenth century could use frailty as a strength. However, it is a strategy which Brontë shows to have devastating consequences.

Edgar's retirement to the library after the confrontation between himself and Heathcliff, and his ignorance of Catherine's illness has been commented upon as part of the conflict between experience and culture in the novel. Edgar counters his interaction with the real by submerging himself in literature. Such a critical position of course assumes that literature is not part of the 'real'.

Catherine's failure to recognise her face in the mirror in this chapter has been noted by many critics, and lends itself particularly to a **psychoanalytic** reading. Her incredulity that Edgar continues to occupy himself with his books while she is dying once more highlights the discrepancy in values between the two houses of Nature and Culture. This agonising perception of dislocation immediately preceedes Catherine's fervent plucking out of the feathers from her pillows:

> That's a turkey's' she murmured to herself; 'and this is a wild duck's; and this is a pigeon's. Ah, they put pigeons' feathers in the pillows – no wonder I couldn't die! Let me take care to throw it on the floor when I lie down. And here is a moorcock's; and this – I should know it among a thousand – it's a lapwing's. Bonny bird; wheeling over our heads in the middle of the moor. It wanted to get to its nest, for the cloud touched the swells, and it felt rain coming. This feather was picked up from the heath, the bird was not shot – we saw its nest in winter, full of little skeletons. Heathcliff set a trap over it, and the old ones dare not come. I made him promise he'd never shoot a lapwing, after that, and he didn't. Yes, here are more! Did he shoot my lapwings, Nelly? Are they red, any of them? Let me look.' (p. 121)

A great deal of critical attention has been paid to this passage which can be read as another allegory, another story about the story. The anecdote of the lapwings prefigures Catherine's own orphaning after her parents die, and prefigures her grave upon the moors. As Joyce Carol Oates notes:

> Her passion for Heathcliff notwithstanding, Catherine's identification is with the frozen and peopleless void of an irrecoverable past, and not with anything human. The feathers she pulls out of her pillow are of course the feathers of dead, wild birds, moorcocks and lapwings: they compel her to think not of the exuberance of childhood, but of death, and even premature death, which is associated with her companion Heathcliff.

Psychoanalytic readings have seen this type of 'madness' identified by Nelly as a 'maniac's' (p. 127) behaviour as both a symptom and effect of oppression.

Gilbert and Gubar see the madness as a result of Catherine's imprisonment:

CHECK THE NET
Use a search engine to find Joyce Carol Oates' article on The Magnanimity of *Wuthering Heights*.

> Imprisonment leads to madness, solipsism, paralysis, as Byron's
> *Prisoner of Chillon*, some of Brontë's Gondal poems, and
> countless other gothic and neo-gothic tales suggest. Starvation –
> both in the modern sense of malnutrition and the archaic
> Miltonic sense of freezing ('to starve in ice') – leads to weakness,
> immobility and death.   (in Rylance, 1987, p. 253)

A **marxist** or **new historicist** critique however, reminds us that
madness is itself ideologically determined. The reference to the pigeon
feathers serves to situate Catherine in a discourse of natural spirituality
or superstition that is in direct conflict with the dominant discourse of
Christianity, which Nelly will invoke upon Catherine's death.

Feminist readings of the passage may read Catherine's madness here
as a function of the conditions of proper femininity, the domesticity
of wifedom and motherhood. Her madness, according to such
readings, is caused precisely by the very aspects of her life that are
supposed to identify her as a 'proper woman'. Thus whilst the story
expresses an absolute social dissatisfaction, and articulates the
mental pain that is its result, it also emphasises the trap of
femininity from which there is no escape.

QUESTION

Give a reading of
the function of
madness in this
novel from either
a marxist or a
feminist
perspective?

CHAPTER 13

- Catherine diagnosed as having brain-fever.
- Edgar nurses her devotedly.
- Letters from Isabella to Edgar and Nelly suggest that she
  quickly regrets her decision to elope with Heathcliff.
- It transpires that they are both now living back at the Heights.
  Isabella is without an ally there, and begs Nelly to call.

For two months Isabella and Heathcliff remain absent. Catherine is
diagnosed as having brain-fever and is nursed devotedly by Edgar,
under whose ministrations she slowly begins to improve. Susan

Sontag has written persuasively about the use of illness as a cultural **metaphor** in *Illness as Metaphor* and *Aids and its Metaphors* (1989): 'Above all, [illness] was a way of affirming the value of being more conscious, more complex, psychologically. Health becomes banal, even vulgar' (p. 26). Sontag continues 'Brain-fever might well be thought of as the disease of someone who is a "creature of passionate extremes, someone too sensitive to bear the horrors of the vulgar everyday world"' (p. 36).

Six weeks after their departure Isabella writes to Edgar a letter which ends with a secret pencilled note begging for reconciliation. He ignores the request. She then writes to Nelly, and Nelly now reads this letter to Lockwood. It commences with the information that Isabella and Heathcliff are back at Wuthering Heights as Hindley is intent on winning back from Heathcliff all the money he has lost to him through gambling. Isabella perceives herself to be both friendless and abused in her relationship with Heathcliff. Hindley shows Isabella a gun with which he intends to kill Heathcliff, and her reaction to this weapon is one of covetousness rather than horror. Heathcliff has heard of Catherine's illness and blames Edgar for it, promising that Isabella shall be her proxy in suffering. The letter and the chapter end with an entreaty from Isabella to Nelly Dean to call on her at Wuthering Heights.

COMMENTARY

The reference to the gun, which Isabella views with desire rather than horror is again indicative that violence is as much a part of the civilised life (which Isabella has hitherto represented) as it is a part of the rude brutality of the Heights. Isabella's devotion to Heathcliff results in her destruction and despair, and this is contrasted both with Edgar's devotion to Catherine, and also Catherine's choice of social status over passion. Isabella's inability to partake of the food at Wuthering Heights because it is too coarse for her can be read as indicative of her unlikeliness to be nourished or sustained by life with Heathcliff.

GLOSSARY

mim prim

minching and munching affected ways

flitting moving house

thible stirring stick or spoon

nave fist

pale t'guilp off skim the froth off

deaved aht knocked out

meeterly properly

mells meddles

madling fool

pining starving

plisky tantrum

CHECK THE BOOK

For a collection of such essays see Mills et al, *Feminist Readings, Feminists Reading* (1989).

Feminist theorists have devoted some attention to the gun which Isabella desires, and the whip requested by Catherine at the beginning if the novel, reading both of these as phallic symbols. It is important to note that as phallic symbols they signify desire not for the penis as such, but for the power the penis represents. As many feminist critics have pointed out, all the economic power in the feudal institution of marriage as it is described in this novel resides with the men.

GLOSSARY

brach she-dog; bitch

dree cheerless

CHAPTER 14

- Nelly goes to see Isabella as requested.
- Heathcliff determines to see Catherine and Nelly reluctantly agrees to act as intermediary.
- Time switches to the present. The doctor calls on Lockwood, and Lockwood reflects that he must be cautious of falling in love with the present Catherine for fear that she should resemble the first.

Nelly informs Edgar of Isabella's predicament, but he refuses to treat her as kin. Nelly pays a visit to Isabella at Wuthering Heights and comments upon the general air of neglect and disrepair. Heathcliff enquires about Catherine and resolves to see her, whether permission is granted or not. Isabella defends Edgar, but is humiliated by Heathcliff, and departs. Nelly is finally prevailed upon by Heathcliff to act as intermediary between himself and Catherine.

At the end of the chapter the narrative is once more restored to Lockwood, and the present, and Lockwood reminds himself that the lesson he must take from Nelly Dean's story is not to fall in love with Catherine Heathcliff, lest she turns out to be another version of her mother.

COMMENTARY

Lockwood typically draws the wrong conclusion from Nelly Dean's story, for Nelly Dean sees marriage to someone else as the only escape for Catherine Heathcliff, and is eager to find her another husband. Lockwood however, represents exactly the supersensitive, precious world of the educated, or cultured which is here contrasted with the world of passion and experience. Lockwood's illness situates him as profoundly disconnected from mundane reality, or daily life. Here Brontë cautions us against identifying too closely with the views of either narrator.

Isabella's position as a dependant upon Heathcliff is made clear in two passages: firstly when Heathcliff asserts the lengths he has gone to in order to prevent Isabella claiming a separation (p. 149). In fact the effort would not have been considerable, since as John Stuart Mill notes in *The Subjection of Women* in 1869, the position of women within marriage was worse than that of slaves. The second passage makes reference to Isabella's mental health (p. 150) and refers to the practice of incarcerating women as mentally ill, notwithstanding any evidence to the contrary. Here we see Brontë's sensitivity to the ways in which power is both mercenary and partial. It is available for appropriation, and Heathcliff makes ample use of this, incarcerating Isabella at Wuthering Heights, keeping her isolated and apart in a duplicate world with special rules over which he has sole control.

 CHECK THE BOOK
John Stuart Mill's *The Subjection of Women* (1869), provides an interesting almost contemporary account of the place and role of women in Victorian society.

VOLUME TWO

CHAPTER 1

Lockwood resumes the narrative only to impersonate that of Nelly Dean.
- The narrative recommences with Heathcliff's visit to Catherine which upon discovery by Edgar reduces Catherine to fainting and further illness.

Nelly returns to Thrushcross Grange and arranges matters so that the household is empty apart from herself and Catherine, in order that Heathcliff might pay his visit. On seeing Catherine, Heathcliff despairs, perceiving that she is certainly going to die. The conversation and interaction between Catherine and Heathcliff ricochets between love and death, and they fall on each other in passionate embrace, while talking of going to the grave. Nelly, nervous that the rest of the members of the household will return and her part in the deception will be exposed, grows anxious for Heathcliff to leave, but Catherine begs him to stay. Catherine faints in Heathcliff's arms just as Edgar Linton enters. When they finally manage to revive Catherine, Heathcliff has departed, but resolves to stay in the garden until Nelly can bring him news of Catherine.

COMMENTARY

Nelly is once again a catalyst for action as she traffics between Wuthering Heights and Thrushcross Grange. The narration which throughout has properly belonged to Lockwood, as the opening to this second volume reminds us, is nevertheless more credibly Nelly Dean's. The opening chapter of this second volume highlights the drama of the conflicts and correspondences between sexuality and death. It is possible to draw parallels between the concerns of this chapter and concerns which dominate Brontë's poetry, not least the longing to escape this world, either through love or death.

CHAPTER 2

- Catherine's daughter Cathy Linton is born the same night, two months prematurely.
- Catherine dies in childbirth.
- Heathcliff knows the news even before Nelly tells him.
- The funeral is held one week later.

That night Catherine goes into labour two months early and gives birth to a daughter, named Catherine after her mother. Catherine, however, dies in childbirth and Edgar is so grieved by Catherine's death that he cannot welcome his daughter. Heathcliff cries that he cannot live without Catherine, she is his life and soul, which echoes her previous declaration of love for him in Chapter 9. Similarly his declaration comes just as she has departed and no action upon it can be taken.

The funeral takes place a week later, and although Hindley Earnshaw is invited, Isabella is not. Catherine is buried on a grassy slope in the corner of the graveyard nearest the moor.

COMMENTARY

Reading retrospectively it is possible to see Heathcliff's despair upon seeing Catherine again being provoked not only by his perception of her certain death, but also by his perception of her pregnancy, since his words are: 'Oh Cathy! Oh, my life! How can I bear it?' (p. 158) and we only have Nelly's interpretation of his anguish as being that Catherine was 'fated, sure to die'. Such a reading would support the position which argues for the structural correspondences between sex and death.

An historical reading of the chapter would also highlight the dangers of childbirth for women in the nineteenth century.

Nelly Dean also comments upon the consequences of Catherine's death for the inheritance laws. Old Mr Linton has bequeathed his property to Isabella and subsequently to her male offspring should Edgar fail to have a son.

C. P. Sanger has commented upon the very detailed knowledge that Brontë displays of the inheritance laws of the nineteenth century. This knowledge is crucial to the plot of *Wuthering Heights* since according to this law Catherine Linton cannot inherit Thrushcross Grange when her father dies. Instead the property automatically passes to the male progeny of Isabella. However, should there be no male progeny, or should that son die, the property would then revert to Catherine Linton. It is for this reason that Heathcliff is so intent upon the marriage between Catherine and Linton, for as his daughter-in-law her property becomes his.

CHECK THE BOOK

For an account of Emily Brontë's understanding of the complex laws of entail, see C. P. Sanger's *The Structure of 'Wuthering Heights'* (1926).

A **marxist** or **new historicist** reading of the manner in which Heathcliff is economically transformed and the impact this has upon his emotional relationship with Catherine could argue that her assertion 'That is not my Heathcliff …I shall love mine yet' (p. 159) sites Heathcliff as an opponent of, and not the embodiment of, bourgeois values.

For the sake of clarity the older Catherine will be referred to as Catherine and the younger as Cathy.

CHAPTER 3

- Hindley Earnshaw dies shortly after Catherine.
- Isabella leaves Heathcliff for the South of England where, a few months later, her son, Linton, is born.
- Heathcliff, now living alone at the Heights with Hareton, learns of his son's birth through the servants' gossip.

The day of the funeral marks the beginning of poor weather. Edgar keeps to his room, and Nelly nurses the sick baby into strength. One evening Isabella bursts in unannounced having run away from Heathcliff. As **marxist-feminist** critic, Lynne Pearce points out in her essay 'Sexual Politics'. When Isabella eventually flees the Heights it is indeed as a battered wife.' (in Mills et al., 1989, p. 36) Pearce draws our attention to the very explicit nature of violence against women in this novel, arguing that it is a 'manifestation of patriarchy by force at its most extreme' (p. 36).

She is en route to the South having fled Heathcliff and the Heights. She throws her wedding ring into the fire and describes the living conditions at the Heights as both physically and morally corrupt. If we are to accept Pearce's reading, then this jettisoning of her wedding ring is not merely a rejection of her marriage to Heathcliff, but a profound rejection of the entire oppressive institution of marriage as experienced by a relatively wealthy middle-class woman in the nineteenth century.

Isabella flees to near London where a few months later she gives birth to a son. Heathcliff learns of his son's birth through servants' gossip. Nelly briefly interrupts the chronology of the narrative to interpose that Isabella dies when her son is twelve. She resumes the chronology with her remark that shortly after Catherine's death Hindley dies, leaving the Heights mortgaged in gambling debts to Heathcliff. Heathcliff now lives alone there with the disinherited Hareton.

COMMENTARY

Heathcliff has now gained control of Wuthering Heights, having arrived as a presumed orphan, and having been humiliated by his lack of proper status. Critics have read this transformation in a number of ways. A marxist reading of it could see it as the triumph of capitalism over a belated feudalism in which competition becomes the new tyranny; since it is only through the acquisition of wealth that Heathcliff manages to move from the margins of society to its centre, infiltrating its institutions of marriage and property ownership and appropriating them for his own ends. A **romanticist** reading of the mutation might emphasise the fact that Heathcliff has transformed his fortunes by virtue of his passionate dedication to the cause of feeding his 'greedy jealousy' for Catherine. Hareton, who should be the Heights' rightful inheritor, is dependent upon Heathcliff, who uses the opportunity to repeat the abuse that he himself suffered as someone of no social property.

Barbara T. Gates has a very detailed account published on the web at Victorian Web.com of her analysis of suicides and burial customs in nineteenth-century England, in which she demonstrates that intimate knowledge of the laws and customs attending to death and burial has profound implications for Brontë's plot:

 CHECK THE NET www. victorianweb.org offers a rich and lucid variety of essays on *Wuthering Heights*.

She argues that Brontë's novel draws freely on laws and customs which post-date the setting of her story (1771–1803). In narrating the details surrounding Hindley Earnshaw's death (1784), for example, she draws upon statutes which relate to early Victorian customs. Although the precise cause of Hindley's death is never determined, all reports claim that he died in a state of drunkenness. Kenneth, who informs Nelly of the death, is clear and claims that he 'died true to his character, drunk as a lord' (p. 184).

CONTEXT

Burial at a cross-roads is the traditional place for suicides, who cannot be buried in consecrated ground.

Heathcliff, when Nelly asks if she may proceed with suitable arrangements for Hindley's funeral. retorts that 'Correctly . . . that fool's body should be buried at the cross-roads, without ceremony of any kind. I happened to leave him ten minutes, yesterday afternoon; and, in that interval, he fastened the two doors of the house against me, and he has spent the night in drinking himself to death deliberately!' (p. 185)

As Gates makes clear in her essay the exact circumstances of Hindley's death, which Brontë records in considerable detail, have important implications for the course of the novel. If Hindley did die drunk and debauched, as both Kenneth and Heathcliff indicate he did, then, according to eighteenth-century law and custom, he would automatically have been considered a suicide, exactly as Heathcliff suggests. Even more significantly, if that were to be the case, his property could legally have been forfeited to the Crown, with nothing left for Hareton and hence nothing left for Heathcliff to employ as a tool in his revenge. It is therefore most likely for this reason that Heathcliff allows Nelly to perform proper burial rights for Hindley, thus relinquishing the immediate gratification of revenge upon Hindley's dead body for the larger rewards of power over the entire Earnshaw family.

Also, it is worth remarking Nelly's disproportionate grief upon hearing of Hindley's death: 'I confess this blow was greater to me than the shock of Mrs Linton's death: ancient associations lingered round my heart; I sat down in the porch and wept as for a blood relation' (p. 184).

Nelly's grief emphasises the tight structural pairings in this novel. Nelly and Hindley, Heathcliff and Catherine and Isabella and Edgar all grow up in more or less fraternal relationships. Nelly's mother was in fact Hindley's wet nurse, so they did literally share 'mother's milk'. With Nelly's grief we see Brontë once again making a critical comparison between genuine heartfelt feelings of loss and grief and the formal requirements of institutionalised religion, reminiscent of the grief demonstrated by Catherine and Heathcliff when their 'father' dies.

CHAPTER 4

- Twelve years pass.
- Edgar receives a letter from Isabella informing him that she is dying and pleading with him to care for her son. He brings Linton home to the Grange at Isabella's request.
- During the time Edgar is away Cathy ventures to Wuthering Heights and meets Hareton.

Nelly describes the next twelve years as being very happy ones, bringing up Cathy who lives a loving and protected life at the Grange, never venturing beyond its boundaries. Edgar receives a letter from Isabella, informing him that she is dying. He complies with her request that he bring her son, Linton, back to the Grange. Edgar is away for three weeks organising Isabella's funeral and Linton's move North. During this time Cathy ventures beyond the confines of the Grange and is eventually tracked down to Wuthering Heights, where she meets Hareton. She is horrified to learn that he too is her cousin. Nelly Dean is very annoyed with Cathy and impresses upon her that she must not inform her father of her newfound knowledge or he might order Nelly to leave his employment.

COMMENTARY

Both the Grange and the Heights can be read as confining spaces, imprisoning this new generation of Lintons and Earnshaws. Hareton is confined by Heathcliff who has cheated him of his inheritance, and has refused him any education; and Cathy is confined by the protective nature of life at the Grange, beyond whose boundaries she is not permitted to wander. Read in terms of the conflict between opposing forces, these confines can be seen as the limits of different kinds of knowledge. Hareton is forbidden knowledge of a formal, literary sort, and Cathy is prohibited from experiencing any life other than that which her father controls. When the two come into confrontation they can neither comprehend nor admit each other.

GLOSSARY
baht without
nowt nothing
maks noa 'cahnt
pays no attention to
norther neither
darr dare

CHAPTER 5

- Isabella dies, Edgar returns with Linton.
- They no sooner arrive back at the Grange than Heathcliff demands Linton's presence at the Heights.
- Edgar is forced to promise to deliver the boy the following day.

The death of Isabella means that Edgar can return to the Grange with his nephew Linton Heathcliff. Linton is described as both sickly and peevish, a delicate and effeminate child. Their arrival back at the Grange is rapidly followed by Joseph, demanding that Linton be returned to his father and Wuthering Heights. Edgar Linton promises to deliver his nephew to the Heights the following day.

COMMENTARY

Linton's description as both sickly and 'effeminate' (p. 198) is further reference to the association of femininity, powerlessness and ill-health. It has been pointed out that according to the rigid structure of the text, Linton Heathcliff is required to be sickly, since he is the offspring of a union that never should have been.

GLOSSARY
mucky dirty

CHAPTER 6

- Nelly takes Linton to Wuthering Heights, where Heathcliff professes his profound disappointment in him.

The next day Nelly is detailed to take Linton to Wuthering Heights, and is bidden not to tell Cathy where he is. Cathy is told only that his father has sent for him suddenly. Linton is reluctant to depart and Nelly tries to soften the blow by preparing him positively for meeting his father and Hareton. Heathcliff is unequivocally disappointed in his son. Heathcliff describes his ambition for Linton as being to take over all the property of both the Lintons and the

Earnshaws. In spite of the vindictive avarice of this ambition, Nelly takes comfort from the thought that in order to achieve it Heathcliff must take care of his son, and provide him with the education that befits a gentleman of property. Linton repeats his mother's inability to eat the food at Wuthering Heights (Volume I, Chapter 13), as it is insufficiently delicate for him. The contrast between Linton and Hareton is pronounced.

COMMENTARY

As Philip K. Wion has noted in his **psychoanalytic** reading of the novel, *Wuthering Heights* is full of oral imagery. Almost all of the social encounters involve food, and food is one of the signs which signals belonging and acceptance. If we persist in the reading of the two houses as representing different kinds of knowledge, then the acceptance of food represents an acceptance of a particular way of understanding life.

Food has also been seen as a sexual metaphor, incorporating as it does, profound oral gratification. A delicate appetite might therefore be read as a reluctance to experience or engage with the sensual or the physical.

Food imagery in *Wuthering Heights* then operates simultaneously as the symbol of care and love, with Nelly frequently offering her charges plates of nourishing comfort food, and the instrument of control and authority. As such it demonstrates neatly the difficulties critics have had in deciding whether this is a love story or a story of social manners.

Clifton Snider's Jungian essay 'The Vampire Archetypes in *Wuthering Heights* and *Jane Eyre*' offers an intriguing analysis of the uses of food and animal imagery in *Wuthering Heights*.

> **CONTEXT**
> Food also has mythic resonance. Accepting food from a someone places you in their power, as Persephone failed to remember when offered the pomegranate. It is not difficult to read the refusal of food in this novel as a refusal of power.

 CHECK THE NET
Use a search engine to find Clifton Snider's essay on vampires and *Wuthering Heights*.

GLOSSARY

nab a jutting hill or rock. Often this term comes to name a particular piece of hill or moorland.

gaumless witless, lacking in understanding

faster more firmly

lath weakling

CHAPTER 7

- Cathy's disappointment at the untimely disappearance of her cousin gives way in time to a resigned acceptance.

- On her sixteenth birthday she encounters Heathcliff and goes back to Wuthering Heights where she sees Linton again and learns of her various relationships.

- She confronts her father with her newfound knowledge.

- She learns of Heathcliff's plans for revenge and agrees not to visit the Heights again, but nevertheless conspires to find a way to correspond with Linton.

The chapter opens with Cathy's disappointment at her cousin's departure. Nelly retains some knowledge of Linton via her relationship with the housekeeper at Wuthering Heights, and although Edgar refuses any contact, he nevertheless encourages Nelly to continue to gain such intelligence. Cathy reaches her sixteenth birthday, and on a trip onto the moors accompanied by Nelly, strays onto Heathcliff's land. She encounters both Heathcliff and Hareton, and much against Nelly's will, Heathcliff prevails upon them to return to Wuthering Heights. Heathcliff reveals his plan to Nelly that the two cousins (Linton and Cathy) should marry. Then, should Linton die, ownership of Thrushcross Grange would devolve to Heathcliff. Cathy sees Linton again and learns of her relationship to both Heathcliff and Hareton. Hareton and Linton are compared and contrasted. Linton and Cathy mock Hareton's lack of knowledge, when it emerges that he cannot read. When Cathy returns home she confronts her father with her newly discovered knowledge and he reveals to her Heathcliff's long-fostered plans for revenge. At the request of her father, Cathy agrees not to return to the Heights, but nevertheless determines to correspond with Linton in spite of this being forbidden. Nelly discovers her secret and threatens to burn the letters or reveal them to Edgar. Cathy chooses the former and ceases the correspondence.

COMMENTARY

Critical attention has frequently focused on the role of textuality and education in this novel, and this chapter highlights these issues. This is a novel which abounds with forbidden texts, from Catherine's diaries through to Cathy's love letters. Text comes to represent knowledge, and Hareton is abused for his lack of it, or for his inability to control it. All the characters in this novel, including its two narrators, are readers in one sense or another, needing to make sense of the signs before them. Nelly Dean uses her knowledge gained from reading to control events in the novel. As Linda Peterson observes in her introduction to a critical edition of *Wuthering Heights*, Brontë seems ambivalent about the effects of education. On the one hand, the denial of education is seen as a form of social punishment; on the other, the conventional forms of nineteenth-century education are frequently pitted against power, both sexual and physical. In this chapter, Brontë's knowledge of the inheritance laws and the implication they have for women's social position is made explicit.

QUESTION

Consider the importance of textuality in this novel.

CHAPTER 8

- Edgar Linton develops a chill.
- Heathcliff again encounters Cathy and informs her that Linton is dying of a broken heart owing to her abrupt termination of their correspondence.
- Cathy sets out again to see Linton.

GLOSSARY
starved frozen
sackless dispirited
canty lively
Slough of Despond a reference to John Bunyan's *Pilgrim's Progress*

The chapter opens with another distinct reference to time, and the seasonal change. Edgar Linton is enfeebled by a chill and is confined indoors. Cathy is left to amuse herself, and sometimes Nelly undertakes to accompany her in her solitude. One day when she and Nelly are out walking, Cathy climbs over a wall and cannot get back. Behind the wall she again encounters Heathcliff who informs her that Linton is dying of a broken heart because she has curtailed all correspondence with him. Cathy's sensitive nature is deeply troubled by both this news and her fears that her father will die of his chill. The next day, she and Nelly set out to pay another visit to Linton.

COMMENTARY

The chapter includes a number of structural elements that have claimed the attention of **formalist** critics. These include: boundaries, illness, death and responsibility.

Heathcliff's information that Linton is dying of a broken heart is disingenuous, since Linton is physically failing and Heathcliff is desirous of rekindling the love affair between Linton and Cathy so that his plans for revenge are not thwarted.

CHAPTER 9

- Cathy and Nelly again visit Wuthering Heights.
- A quarrel about the nature of marriage.
- Linton persuades Cathy to return the following day, and because Nelly too falls ill with a chill, Cathy is able to visit Linton unimpaired by any restrictive supervision.

The following day Cathy and Nelly again visit the Heights to find Linton more peevish and delicate than ever. Cathy and Linton quarrel about the nature of marriage. During the quarrel Cathy tells Linton that his parents hated each other, and he informs her that her mother hated her father and loved his. Linton's triumph is succeeded by a prolonged coughing fit which causes both Nelly and Cathy concern. By wheedling and whining and prevailing upon Cathy's sensitive nature, Linton secures a promise from her that she will come and visit him again, a promise Cathy is able to keep because Nelly falls ill with a chill and can no longer supervise her movements.

COMMENTARY

Here illness is once more cited as a strategy. It is used effectively by
Linton to influence Cathy's movements, and Nelly's chill is an
unwitting factor in Cathy's secret visits to the Heights.

CHAPTER 10

- Three weeks later Nelly is restored to health, much to Cathy's
  frustration.
- Nelly discovers Cathy's deception.
- Discussion of ideal heaven between Linton and Cathy.
- Hareton's attempts to read again the subject of mockery.
- Nelly informs Edgar of Cathy's visits, which are promptly
  curtailed.

GLOSSARY
frame invent
throstles thrushes
coned learned
sarve ye aht take
revenge; serve you
right
skift move
bahn going, here
bound

Once again the chapter opens with a definite reference to time.
Nelly is recovered from her chill and requires Cathy to read to her,
which interferes with Cathy's secret visits to the Heights. Nelly
discovers her secret, and Cathy confides in her the details of all her
visits, most of which have been dutiful rather than pleasurable. She
recounts an argument that she and Linton have had about the nature
of heaven, in which she accuses his vision of being only 'half alive'
and he accuses hers of being 'drunk' (p. 245).

Cathy also relates a conversation with Hareton in which he
attempts to impress her with his newly acquired knowledge of
reading, and she is once more scornful of the limits of his
knowledge. For this Nelly reproves her.

Nelly betrays Cathy's confidence and informs Edgar of her
behaviour, and Edgar forbids Cathy to visit the Heights again.
However, he writes to his nephew and invites him to the
Grange.

QUESTION

Consider the relationships between knowledge and character in this novel.

COMMENTARY

The chapter expands upon one of the central themes of the novel: the nature and uses of knowledge. Hareton is abused for his limited skills; Nelly Dean uses her knowledge to influence events in the novel – her betrayal of Cathy's confidences has profound consequences for the health of both Edgar and Linton, though she is unaware of this as a consequence. Critics interested in the gender issues of this novel have commented upon this emphasis on Edgar and Linton's illnesses as serving to feminise them.

The argument about heaven is indicative of a reversal in the natures of the Grange and the Heights, since Linton's view is constricted and peaceful, and Cathy's sparkles and dances 'in a glorious jubilee' (p. 245) suggesting that neither Linton nor Cathy are where they properly belong.

CHAPTER 11

- Edgar, realising his death is imminent, commences a correspondence with Linton in an attempt to reassure himself of Cathy's future.

The chapter opens with a move of the narrative back to the present.

Nelly perceives Lockwood's fascination with Cathy, but when Lockwood forestalls her conjecture, she resumes her story once more, though even this part of her story is more contemporary, the events having happened only in the last year.

Lockwood's denial of his interest in Cathy at this point structurally repeats his account of his refusal of a 'most fascinating creature, a real goddess' (Vol. 1, Ch. 1, p. 6) at the beginning of the novel. His interest in women is relentlessly scopic or voyeuristic. With the exception of his relationship with Nelly Dean his interaction with women is both awkward and stilted. He is frequently to be caught peeping at them through doorways or windows, and his fantasized interactions with them are almost always demonstrated to be vainglorious.

Edgar knows that his health is failing and grows increasingly concerned about Cathy's future. He is torn between wishing to die in order to be reunited with Catherine, and fearing abandoning Cathy to the weak son of Heathcliff. Accordingly Edgar begins a correspondence with Linton, Linton's part in which is closely supervised by Heathcliff. Linton too is dying, but Heathcliff conceals this knowledge and is anxious to get a wedding arranged before his chance disappears. No one at Thrushcross Grange suspects Linton's health to be as precarious as it actually is.

COMMENTARY

Once again letters play a critical and unreliable part in the sequence of events. Edgar is deceived by the letters Linton sends him into thinking that his nephew is healthier than he really is.

Edgar's confession to Nelly that he has been happy with his 'little Cathy' (p. 254) is reminiscent of Catherine's remonstrances to Heathcliff when she is dying: 'will you be happy when I am in the earth?' (Vol. 2, Ch. 1, p. 158). Read in the light of this it is not so much an acknowledgement of his love of his daughter as a confession of his insufficient love of Catherine.

CHECK THE BOOK

In her book *Victorian Writing and Working Women* (1985) Julia Swindells offers an interesting account of the relationships between medicine, health and power in the nineteenth century.

CHAPTER 12

- Cathy and Linton meet on the moors and it is clear that Linton's health is failing, a fact which she conceals from her father when she returns home.

Another chapter which opens with a specific reference to time. Cathy and Nelly set out in late summer to meet Linton on the moors. They are astonished and alarmed at his ill-health. Linton is clearly unable to enjoy the meeting but begs Cathy to stay, and also to report to her father that she has found him in tolerable health. Linton is exhausted by the interchange and falls asleep. When he awakens he is confused and beset by voices which torment him, primarily his father's. Once he is awake, Cathy and Nelly feel able to leave him and to return to the Grange. Following Nelly's inclination they erroneously decide to keep from Edgar the extent of his nephew's ill-health.

COMMENTARY

In this chapter we are again confronted with a narrator who is unable or unwilling to read the signs. Nelly perceives that Linton is seriously enfeebled but permits neither herself nor Edgar that knowledge. This reluctance to acknowledge Linton's illness has disastrous consequences for Cathy. Nelly's refusal to acknowledge the gravity of Linton's illness exactly reiterates her earlier fatal mistake to acknowledge Catherine's malady.

GLOSSARY
ling heather
bespeak beg for
eft small lizard-like animal

CHAPTER 13

- Cathy and Nelly repeat their meeting with Linton on the moors.
- Linton acts as a decoy to get Cathy and Nelly back to the Heights.
- Heathcliff appears and reveals that he only cares that Linton should outlive Edgar.
- Cathy and Nelly are kept prisoner at Wuthering Heights.

QUESTION

Is *Wuthering Heights* a fairytale, a gothic romance or a novel of domestic realism?

The following week Cathy and Nelly once again meet Linton on the moors as arranged. Edgar is by now reconciled to the union between the two cousins. This meeting, like the last, is fraught with conflict. Cathy knows she is being manipulated by Linton, but she does not understand why. Linton's terror of Heathcliff is manifest, and when Heathcliff appears on the scene he is remorselessly angry with Linton. Heathcliff confides to Nelly that his only desire is that Linton should outlive Edgar. By degrees Cathy and Nelly are persuaded back to the Heights, whereupon Heathcliff takes them prisoner. Once back at the Heights, Linton visibly improves and it is clear that his part in the plan has succeeded. Cathy bites and scratches Heathcliff in her attempt to wrest the keys from him, and his response is to beat her thoroughly, much to Nelly's indignation. Heathcliff's plan is that the two cousins should marry in the morning. Cathy pleads with Heathcliff to be permitted to return to the Grange and promises to marry Linton in return, but Heathcliff refuses her request and tells her that her father must die alone. At this point the novel appears to recall its fairytale status and rehearses some of the structures of traditional fairytales such as Beauty and the Beast, thus re-emphasising the oppressive nature of the marriage contract for women in the nineteenth century.

Nelly and Catherine miss their chance of escape when three servants from the Grange come seeking them, and they are kept imprisoned for the next four days.

Nelly reveals her legal and clerical knowledge when she reminds Heathcliff that his crime is 'felony without benefit of clergy' (p. 271).

> **CONTEXT**
>
> Nelly's reference is to the system of laws which exempt clergy from civil prosecution for certain crimes. Her point here is that Heathcliff's crime is so heinous that there will be no escape-clause to which he might appeal for mercy.

CHAPTER 14

- On the fifth day Nelly is able to return to the Grange where Edgar is barely alive.
- She informs Edgar of Heathcliff's plan and Edgar decides to change his will.
- However, the lawyer arrives too late, but Cathy arrives back just in time to witness her father's dying moments.

Five days into their imprisonment Zillah reveals that the official story is that Cathy and Nelly had been sunk in the marsh for five days until Heathcliff had rescued them. She also informs them that although Edgar is not yet dead he is not expected to last longer than another day. Nelly is able to return to the Grange, but cannot find Cathy, who has been married to Linton in the meantime. Nelly therefore returns alone to the Grange and informs Edgar that both she and Cathy are alive and well, and she implements plans to return with a rescue party to Wuthering Heights so that they might rescue Cathy. She tells Edgar of Heathcliff's revenge, and Edgar resolves to change his will so that his property can be held in trust for Cathy and her children, rather than devolving to Heathcliff. However, the lawyer arrives too late and Edgar dies without being able to change his will. He does not die, however, before Cathy returns. So the will remains unchanged and Cathy's fate seems sealed. Edgar dies with his daughter at his side. It emerges that the lawyer has been bribed by Heathcliff to ignore Edgar Linton's summons.

COMMENTARY

Since Edgar Linton fails to change his will and tie up his property in trusts, Linton is correct in his odious assumption that all Cathy's property now belongs to him (p. 277).

? QUESTION

Consider Brontë's use of power relationships in this novel with reference to two of the following;

• property laws
• medicine
• literacy
• social class
• gender.

CHAPTER 15

• Heathcliff demands that Cathy return to the Heights since he intends to put a tenant in the Grange.

• He reveals his plans to be buried in the same space as Catherine, and tells Nelly how she has haunted him over the years.

• He returns to the Heights with Cathy leaving Nelly alone at the Grange.

After the funeral of her father Cathy and Nelly remain at the Grange, but before long Heathcliff arrives and as master of the property informs Cathy that she must return as his dependent to the Heights. He outlines his intention to put a tenant in the Grange. As Cathy collects her belongings, Heathcliff divulges to Nelly his intention to be buried alongside Catherine, in the same coffin-space, so that when Edgar's body finally merges with hers she and Heathcliff will already be merged together. Heathcliff and Cathy leave for the Heights leaving Nelly at the Grange.

COMMENTARY

Critical attention has focused on the transgressive nature of this chapter. Certainly, Heathcliff's description of his plan to merge with Catherine is grisly, and equally it is a plan which transgresses the boundary between life and death, and between propriety and necrophilia. As Nancy Armstrong (in Stoneman, 1993) observes in her essay 'Brontë in and out of her Time' Heathcliff's plan can be interpreted as an occult dramatisation of a demonic love which utterly defies the conventions of nineteenth-century romance.

CHAPTER 16

- Linton dies, and Cathy is too proud to accept the offers of friendship from either Hareton or Zillah, so she remains isolated at the Heights.

Since Cathy's forced removal by Heathcliff to Wuthering Heights, Nelly has not seen her, but she learns odd morsels of information from Zillah, whom she sees from time to time. When Cathy arrives she is bidden to look after Linton until he dies – a task for which she feels herself to be very ill equipped. When Linton dies, Cathy remains upstairs in her room for a fortnight refusing every gesture of kindness from Zillah and Hareton, both of whom would be willing to offer her more friendship were she not so proud. Nelly Dean's story ends here, with her unable to foresee any kind of future for Cathy unless she is able to remarry. The narrative thus passes back to Lockwood, who reveals his intention to give up his tenancy of the Grange in October.

COMMENTARY

Since Linton is a minor when he dies, he cannot will the lands that he inherits by marrying Cathy to his father, but Heathcliff claims a right to them in any case. Cathy's position as a dispossessed widow radically disables her from contesting Heathcliff's command of the property and land.

GLOSSARY

thrang busy

train-oil whale-oil (for cleaning guns)

that road in that direction, as far as that is concerned

taking rage

stalled of tired of

GLOSSARY

Chevy Chase a medieval English ballad

causeway a cobbled area, pavement

CHAPTER 17

- Narrative returns to Lockwood and the present day.
- Lockwood takes a note to Cathy from Nelly, and reveals to Heathcliff that he has come to terminate his tenancy.

With the resumption of the narratorial position, Lockwood brings the narrative back to the present day. He agrees to take a note from Nelly to Cathy at the Heights. Once again he is rudely received by both Hareton and Cathy. Lockwood's clumsy attempt to pass Nelly's note secretly to Cathy is thwarted by her assumption that it is a love note. When she eventually learns of the real author of the letter she is filled with reminiscent longing.

Once again Cathy scorns Hareton's attempts to improve his education. Eventually Hareton throws all his books upon the fire, much to his own distress. As Hareton blunders out of the room he collides with Heathcliff, who professes his pleasure at receiving Lockwood again. Lockwood however apprises him of his plans to terminate his tenancy of the Grange. The chapter ends with his self-conceited reflection:

> What a realisation of something more romantic than a fairytale it would have been for Mrs Linton Heathcliff, had she and I struck up an attachment as her good nurse desired, and migrated together, into the stirring atmosphere of the town. (p. 301)

COMMENTARY

Lockwood's deferral of real relationships in favour of the **romantic** dream have already been commented upon from the first chapter wherein he reports his holiday infatuation with his 'goddess'. He can only contemplate the (fairytale) relationship with Cathy once it is clear to him that this is an impossibility. As Margaret Homans (in Peterson, 1992) notes in her **feminist** reading of the novel: 'Lockwood's … entire narrative is predicated on romantic desires, endless oscillations of approach and avoidance'. (p. 345).

CHECK THE BOOK

See Emily Brontë's 1841 poem 'I do not weep, I would not weep' which refers to the comfort derived from a belief in the afterlife.

Once again Brontë reiterates the tensions and difficulties of acquiring valuable knowledge: Cathy jettisons her chance, and Hareton likewise jettisons his own, much to their individual distress.

CHAPTER 18

- 1802. Lockwood happens to be in the locality again and is seized by the impulse to visit the Grange.
- He also visits the Heights where a picture of domestic bliss greets him.
- Nelly Dean receives him warmly and tells him that Heathcliff is dead.

GLOSSARY

frough from

wick week

mensful decent

haulf half

sartin certain

fellies male admirers

jocks jugs

side out of t'gait get out of the way

it ull be mitch you'll be lucky

This is the second chapter to open with a date, and structurally it repeats and revises the first. Lockwood is travelling in the area again and decides to pay a visit to both the Grange and the Heights. When he arrives at Wuthering Heights he peeps in through the windows to observe a scene of domestic harmony in which a beautiful young woman, Cathy, is teaching a handsome young man, Hareton, how to read. Lockwood chooses to go in via the servants' entrance whereupon he is joyfully received by Nelly Dean. Nelly informs him of Heathcliff's death some three months since, which she describes as a 'queer end' (p. 306).

COMMENTARY

The narration now passes back to Nelly and she describes for Lockwood the developing relationship between Hareton and Cathy. The relationship has been conducted around learning, both in terms of Hareton's acquisition of literacy skills, and Cathy's developing humility.

Critics have tended to see this relationship between Cathy and Hareton as the resolution of all the conflicts of the novel, though opinion is divided as to whether the relationship constitutes a successful resolution.

GLOSSARY

lug carry

yah muh bend tuh th'yoak you may bend to the yolk; i.e., you can put up with her ways

een eyes

mattock garden implement

CHAPTER 19

- Cathy and Hareton begin to negotiate their relationship under the hostile eyes of Joseph and Heathcliff.
- Heathcliff's will for revenge has diminished now that it lies within his power.
- Heathcliff desires to die in order to be reunited with Catherine, but feels himself to be trapped within a healthy body.

Nelly recommences her narrative with a description of how Hareton and Cathy begin to form their friendship, and the implications that their friendship has for the political structure of the household. An anecdote about them digging up Joseph's prized blackcurrant bushes in order to plant flowers is indicative of Cathy's will to cultivate the garden, and transform the Heights from a utilitarian place into a place for pleasure. Readings of the novel which see Cathy's relationship with Hareton as the resolution of the dissonance between the two houses, might wish to explore the planting of flowers as the integration of nature and culture implied in the term cultivation. The flowers are described as an 'importation of plants from the Grange' (p. 314) and thus are suggestive of Cathy's own position, scion of Catherine, imported from the Grange to her truly native soil. That she is displacing Joseph's blackcurrant bushes is indicative of the fact that his way of life must now give way to a new generation.

COMMENTARY

Her new-found friendship with Hareton gives Cathy the confidence to rebel against Heathcliff's tyranny. But Heathcliff has abandoned his plans for revenge and is desirous only of dying. The whole world seems to be constructed of memorabilia of Catherine, and Heathcliff feels trapped in a body which refuses to die, whereas his soul is already 'in the grave' (Vol. 2, Ch.1, p. 161). The rhetoric of this quotation has its origins in Emily Brontë's poetry.

J. Hillis Miller's **deconstructive** reading of the novel particularly focuses attention on the emphasis in this chapter upon memorabilia.

CHECK THE BOOK

Emily Brontë: *The Complete Poems* (1995, reprint, p. 29) demonstrates the links between this passage and Brontë's poetry.

He argues that each thing that Heathcliff encounters reminds him not of Catherine, but of his loss of Catherine. Like all texts, the memoranda are thus a memoranda to absence, not to presence: they are a tormenting reminder to Heathcliff of his failure to possess Catherine. Miller draws the parallel between this and the act of storytelling, which he observes is always after the event, it is always constructed over a loss. With its dual narration highlighting the loss of the oral tradition of storytelling this novel might be said to be doubly constructed about a loss.

CHAPTER 20

- Heathcliff is obsessed with dying.
- Finally he dies threatening Nelly that if she does not bury his body according to his wishes he will haunt her forever.

GLOSSARY

rare and pleased highly delighted

chuck a term of endearment

girning grinning or grimacing: the rictus smile of death

Heathcliff's behaviour grows increasingly bizarre and he disappears for days at a time. When he returns, he returns in a glittery, strangely joyful mood. His manner quite discomfits Nelly, who is superstitious about ghosts and the inexplicable. When his conversation turns to making out a will, Nelly tries to convince him to repent of his former ways and turn to God. He threatens to haunt her if she does not see that his body is buried according to his wishes. Two days later she finds him dead. Hareton, who has been the most wronged by Heathcliff, is the only person who really mourns his loss. Heathcliff is buried according to his desires, against the opened side of Catherine's coffin. Local legend has it that their ghosts still walk the moors. So Lockwood hears the end of the story and on walking past the graveyard on his way home, pauses to wonder: 'how anyone could ever imagine unquiet slumbers for the sleepers in that quiet earth' (p. 334). This reveals not only Lockwood's peculiar lack of imagination, but also his continued inability to comprehend the signs of the landscape in which he moves.

QUESTION

How useful is
Lockwood as a
narrator in
*Wuthering
Heights*?

COMMENTARY

The last chapter again revisits the conflict between ethical
convention and a higher morality associated with consummate
passion.

Lockwood's continued incompetence as a reader of signs throws
into disarray all his assumptions as narrator throughout the novel,
causing us to reconsider his judgements again.

EXTENDED COMMENTARIES

This section takes a number of passages from *Wuthering Heights*
and offers a sample analysis of the passages from a variety of critical
positions. The purpose is to demonstrate that there is no one
literary theory, or position from which some absolutely totalisable,
comprehensible understanding of the text can be arrived at. Rather
there are many models of thought, ways of reading, processes of
understanding, which can overlap and contrast with each other.
What follows is not an exercise in how to produce a 'perfect'
feminist or **psychoanalytical** reading. It offers something
potentially more fascinating and rewarding: which is, showing
how a text might be read so as to spark many different insights
and connections in the reader's mind.

TEXT 1 (PAGES 80–1)

'I was only going to say that heaven did not seem to be my
home; and I broke my heart with weeping to come back to earth;
and the angels were so angry that they flung me out, into the
middle of the heath on the top of Wuthering Heights; where I
woke sobbing for joy ... I've no more business to marry Edgar
Linton than I have to be in heaven; and if the wicked man in
there had not brought Heathcliff so low, I shouldn't have
thought of it. It would degrade me to marry Heathcliff, now; so
he shall never know how I love him; and that, not because he's
handsome, Nelly, but because he's more myself than I am.
Whatever our souls are made of, his and mine are the same, and

Linton's is as different as a moonbeam from lightning, or frost from fire.'

Ere this speech ended I became sensible of Heathcliff's presence. Having noticed a slight movement, I turned my head, and saw him rise from the bench and steal out, noiselessly. He had listened till he heard Catherine say it would degrade her to marry him, and then he staid to hear no farther …

'… Heathcliff has no notion of these things … He does not know what being in love is?'

'I see no reason that he should not know, as well as you,' I returned; 'and if you are his choice, he'll be the most unfortunate creature that ever was born! As soon as you become Mrs Linton, he loses friend, and love, and all! Have you considered how you'll bear the separation, and how he'll bear to be quite deserted in the world? Because, Miss Catherine –'

'He quite deserted! we separated!' she exclaimed, with an accent of indignation. 'Who is to separate us, pray? They'll meet the fate of Milo! Not as long as I live, Ellen – for no mortal creature. Every Linton on the face of the earth might melt into nothing, before I could consent to forsake Heathcliff. Oh, that's not what I intend – that's not what I mean! I shouldn't be Mrs Linton were such a price demanded! He'll be as much to me as he has been all his lifetime. Edgar must shake off his antipathy, and tolerate him, at least. He will when he learns my true feelings towards him. Nelly, I see now, you think me a selfish wretch, but, did it never strike you that, if Heathcliff and I married, we should be beggars? whereas, if I marry Linton, I can aid Heathcliff to rise, and place him out of my brother's power … This is for the sake of one who comprehends in his person my feelings to Edgar and myself. I cannot express it; but surely you and every body have a notion that there is, or should be, an existence of yours beyond you. What were the use of creation if I were entirely contained here? My great miseries in this world have been Heathcliff's miseries, and I watched and felt each from the beginning; my great thought in living is himself. If all else perished, and he remained, I should still continue to be; and if all else remained, and he were annihilated, the Universe would turn

QUESTION

Is the love between Catherine and Heathcliff an example of moral magnificence or turpitude?

to a mighty stranger. I should not seem a part of it. My love for Linton is like the foliage in the woods. Time will change it, I'm well aware, as winter changes the trees – my love for Heathcliff resembles the eternal rocks beneath – a source of little visible delight, but necessary. Nelly, I *am* Heathcliff – he's always, always in my mind – not as a pleasure, any more than I am always a pleasure to myself – but as my own being – so don't talk of our separation again – it is impracticable; and –'

Possibly the most famous passage in the novel, Catherine here declares her love for Heathcliff in the most extravagant and arresting of terms.

The passage highlights some of the central thematic oppositions in the novel: joy and redemption; belonging and exclusion; constancy and transience; expediency and struggle. These oppositions contend against each other in an unresolvable tension throughout the novel.

This passage can be seen to deal with issues of identity and individuality, and it does so in cosmological and religious terms. Brontë wrestles with the profoundly existential question of what happens to the notion of the individual when one is in love? It is a question of wide-ranging theological and social implications. The union between herself and Heathcliff Catherine perceives to preclude her from a traditional, authorised Christian version of heaven, and although she suggests that it similarly precludes her from marriage to Edgar Linton, she ignores this and goes on to detail an elaborate rationalisation of her proposed marriage. Such a rationalisation, while it is in direct conflict with her passion for Heathcliff, and threatens to annihilate him, is nevertheless entirely within the bounds of propriety associated with the social contract of marriage. As a daughter who could not expect to inherit any property, Catherine rightly comments that her economic and social survival depends on marriage. The central choice of the novel, then can be read as a stark choice about survival. Catherine recognises that without Heathcliff she could not exist as herself, but that without a legitimate social role and position neither she nor Heathcliff could live.

QUESTION

Is *Wuthering Heights* a moral novel?

It is worth paying some attention to Catherine's response to a Christian heaven, for it prefigures Heathcliff's assertion at the end of the novel that he is 'within sight of [his] heaven' (Vol. 2, Ch. 20, p. 325). As with Lockwood's first dream, and Joseph's sanctimonious moralising, Brontë seems clear in her writing against the traditional, authoritative discourse of Christianity. It is scant wonder then that the novel's contemporary reception viewed it as profoundly immoral.

Catherine's outburst is framed in typically poetic and cosmological terms, her assertion that were Heathcliff to be annihilated the Universe would turn to a mighty stranger seems to echo Brontë's poem 'No Coward Soul'.

CHECK THE BOOK
'No Coward Soul' Can be found in Emily Brontë: *The Complete Poems* (1995, reprint, p. 182).

Feminist and **new historicist** readings of this passage see Brontë as writing directly against the grain of the dominant discourses of the culture in which she lived. She was the daughter of a parson, elaborating a version of Heaven that incorporates and celebrates passion, and denouncing the conventional Christian version. Her very articulation of such a notion places her beyond the pale. Christian tradition held the virtues of silence, obedience and reticence as particularly, maybe even essentially feminine. Marina Warner (1994) makes the argument very powerfully in her analysis of the development of fairy tales *From the Beast to the Blonde*:

> Catholics and Protestants were in agreement: garrulousness was a woman's vice, and silence – which was not even considered an appropriate virtue in the male – one of the chief ornaments a good woman should cultivate. (p. 30)

The articulate woman is a woman who refuses subjection, and rejects her identity as a passive object of desire.

Following this formulation of Christian virtue, speaking implied unruliness and disobedience.

Catherine's declaration of love for Heathcliff, which formulates a passion that goes beyond the boundaries of conventional relationships, threatens the very basis of marriage within the

Christian faith, which she is proposing simply as a means of security. Nelly's response is both shocked and unequivocal: Catherine's is a proposal that is doomed to failure.

Although this is the most dramatic instance of these issues, it is not the only intimation that the ideal relationship cannot be sustained. It echoes Lockwood's confession of being unworthy of a comfortable home in Volume I, Chapter 1 (p. 6), and it is also given its inversion in Isabella's fantastic declaration of the potential of her relationship with Heathcliff in Volume 1, Chapter 10, (pp. 100–3).

CHECK THE BOOK

Elaine Showalter, *Sexual Anarchy* (1991) offers a clear account of the debate.

Feminist readings of the novel have devoted much careful attention to this passage. In the mid to late Victorian period, in which Brontë was writing, there was a fierce debate in the definition of gender, and one of the most hotly contested issues was that of the meaning, and the proper place of women in society Brontë challenges the binary oppositions of man and woman, which give rise to their proper meanings, and she does so at every level. In *Wuthering Heights* it is not that male and female, culture and nature, calm and storm operate as precise opposites. Rather they exist in an uneasy dialectic or tension, jostling for space and stability. Just as Brontë disrupts the dominant Christian formulations of what are proper character traits for a woman, she similarly disturbs conventional binary assumptions that nature belongs to the realm of the female, and culture to the male.

Catherine passionately committed to nature, nevertheless lives in the midst of the culture that defines her. She is central to its perpetuation as a woman, as an object of exchange within the social contract of marriage. But that centrality is also a form of marginality, since she is always subject to her husband's demands, obedient to his desires and silenced by his authority.

In Catherine and Isabella, Brontë offers a radical challenge to these conventional assumptions, since rather than being offered in marriage by their fathers, as part of an economic transaction, they both attempt to manipulate the parameters of the exchange. Nevertheless, this manipulation is doomed to failure, since the dominant discourses require their submission, a submission which can be read as ultimately leading to their deaths.

Equally, the desire that characterises the love between Catherine and Heathcliff is outside the realm of culture; it is described as having no need of words, it is beyond language; the passion that typifies it situates it as a natural attraction. Catherine's vocabulary as she describes it is anchored in the poetics of the natural world. Her descriptions are all metaphorical.

It is precisely Heathcliff's marginal status – the fact that he never quite belongs to the cultured world of other men – that makes him so attractive to both Catherine and Isabella. He represents the possibility of a love that transgresses all the boundaries.

Catherine and Heathcliff are situated between nature and culture, they participate in both and owe an allegiance to neither, and are thereby able to break down the hierarchy implicit in such binary oppositions.

Nor does Catherine perceive their situation to be unusual. Although it is a commonplace of criticism of this novel to see the relationship between Catherine and Heathcliff as unique and extraordinary, Catherine here is explicit:

> I cannot express it; but surely you and every body have a notion that there is, or should be, an existence of yours beyond you. What were the use of creation if I were entirely contained here?
>
> (Vol. 1. Ch. 9, p. 81)

CHECK THE NET

Search **http:// enotes.com/ wuthering** for a comprehensive resource on the novel.

TEXT 2 (PAGE 79)

'Nelly, do you never dream queer dreams?' She said, suddenly, after some minutes' reflection.

'Yes, now and then,' I answered.

'And so do I. I've dreamt in my life dreams that have stayed with me ever after, and changed my ideas; they've gone through and through me, like wine through water, and altered the colour of my mind. And this is one – I'm going to tell it – but take care not to smile at any part of it.'

'Oh! Don't, Miss Catherine!' I cried. 'We're dismal enough without conjuring up ghosts, and visions to perplex us. Come, come, be merry, and like yourself! Look at little Hareton – *he's* dreaming nothing dreary. How sweetly he smiles in his sleep!'

'Yes; and how sweetly his father curses in his solitude! You remember him, I dare say, when he was just such another as that chubby thing – nearly as young and innocent. However, Nelly, I shall oblige you to listen – it's not long; and I've no power to be merry tonight.'

'I won't hear it, I won't hear it!' I repeated, hastily.

I was superstitious about dreams then, and am still; and Catherine had an unusual gloom in her aspect that made me dread something from which I might shape a prophecy, and foresee a fearful catastrophe.

She was vexed, but she did not proceed.

This passage with its emphasis upon the potency of dreaming is a critical one in terms of how we might respond to the novel. Here the dream, like the central love story of the novel, is endlessly deferred and resisted. Appropriately emotions run high and they are contradictory. Catherine counsels Nelly not to smile at her dream, though Nelly's instinctive reaction is that the dream will provoke dismay and perplexity, not mirth. It is also worth noting that the reason Nelly fears this dream is that she suspects that it will prompt her to prophesy. Nelly's rejection of the dream comes from her percipience rather than her ignorance. Once again we see Nelly as a source of knowledge that runs counter to religious or scientific orthodoxy.

QUESTION

Consider the function of dreams in this novel.

This passage evidently lends itself to a **psychoanalytical** reading. The power of psychoanalytical criticism is that it focuses serious attention upon the text itself, as opposed to its cultural context or the biography of its author. In psychoanalytic theory meaning is to be revealed through a careful analysis of the internal contradictions or slippages within the text. Terry Eagleton (1983) makes the point neatly in his *Literary Theory*:

> By attending to what may seem like evasions, ambivalences and points of intensity in the narrative ... [literary criticism] can begin to probe through the layers of secondary revision and expose something of the 'sub-text' which ... the work both conceals and reveals.
>
> (p. 182)

As a method of literary criticism, psychoanalysis has gone through several transformations. Because it is itself a kind of interpretation, it lends itself to a **hermeneutic** approach to literature, in which the critic, like the analyst, searches the text for clues to its repressed meanings.

It is a mode of criticism gives us the means by which we can open a text out to read complex metaphorical readings. *The Interpretation of Dreams* is generally taken to be Freud's major and most original work. In it Freud investigates dreams, and the phenomenon of dreaming, as the products of a conflictual dialogue between the conscious and unconscious processes of thought. Freud read the obscure discourse of dreams as coded narratives of the ways in which the unconscious mind is conditioned by childhood events. His discoveries form part of a philosophical tradition which sees the human subject as entirely produced by the multiple discourses in which it is entrenched, rather than as autonomous and self-determining.

CHECK THE BOOK

In *The Interpretation of Dreams*, Sigmund Freud (1953) offers a detailed investigation of the function of dreams, and the relationship between dreams and thoughts.

The dream in this passage retains its potency precisely because of its repression. Its impact is perceived via its denials. Catherine has physically to hold Nelly Dean down in order to make her listen to the dream, but she commences the account with its denial and her declaration of the conflict between her feelings for Edgar Linton and Heathcliff which mark the central turning point of the novel:

> 'This is nothing,' cried she; 'I was only going to say that heaven did not seem to be my home; and I broke my heart with weeping to come back to earth; and the angels were so angry that they flung me out, into the middle of the heath on the top of Wuthering Heights; where I woke, sobbing for joy. That will do to explain my secret as well as the other. I've no more business to

marry Edgar Linton than I have to be in heaven; and if the wicked man in there had not brought Heathcliff so low, I shouldn't have thought of it. It would degrade me to marry Heathcliff, now; so he shall never know how I love him; and that, not because he's handsome Nelly, but because he's more myself than I am. Whatever our souls are made of, his and mine are the same, and Linton's is as different as a moonbeam from lightening or frost from fire.'

(Vol. 1, Ch. 9, p. 80)

Catherine's desires, as expressed in this dream, are tacitly acknowledged to be immoral. They unfit her for heaven. The dream is offered as a means of explaining a secret. There are layers of unspoken desires here, and it is precisely this sense of a multi-layered emotional ambiguity within language that makes for such a rich psychoanalytical reading.

Desire in this dream is revealed as the desire for the perverse and the unattainable. Because Edgar Linton is incorporated into the structures of allowable desire, he becomes, perversely, less attractive, which shifts the locus of attraction back again to Heathcliff. For Brontë desire is not directed at any obtainable object at all, however superficially charming it might be. Desire exists in transgression and the satisfaction of desire is death.

Psychoanalytic critics believe that this desperate desire to recover a wholeness experienced as 'lost' can help explain not only why we fall in love, but also why we look for unity in works of art and yearn for 'universal values'. As theorists come to recognise its importance in human motivation, they have increasingly focused attention on what Freud called the pre-Oedipal and Lacan the pre-symbolic.

CHECK THE BOOK

Women: The Longest Revolution by Juliet Mitchell (1984), offers a cogent argument for the enduring potency of *Wuthering Heights*.

Juliet Mitchell (1984) argues persuasively that a psychoanalytic reading explains why the severely limited world of *Wuthering Heights* strikes readers as having a 'cosmic' quality: for her,

the nature and actions of every character in the drama are fully intelligible because they are always related to ... what we now know to be the most critical phase of life: childhood.

(pp. 143–4)

TEXT 3 (PAGES 164–5)

About twelve o'clock, that night, was born the Catherine you saw at Wuthering Heights, a puny seven months' child; and two hours after the mother died, having never recovered sufficient consciousness to miss Heathcliff, or know Edgar.

The latter's distraction at his bereavement is a subject too painful to be dwelt on; its after effects showed how deep the sorrow sunk.

A great addition, in my eyes, was his being left without an heir. I bemoaned that, as I gazed on the feeble orphan; and I mentally abused old Linton for, what was only natural partiality, the securing of his estate to his own daughter, instead of his son's.

An unwelcome infant it was, poor thing! It might have wailed out of life, and nobody cared a morsel, during those first hours of existence. We redeemed the neglect afterwards; but its beginning was as friendless as its end is likely to be.

Next morning – bright and cheerful out of doors – stole softened in through the blinds of the silent room and suffused the couch and its occupant with a mellow, tender glow.

Edgar Linton had his head laid on the pillow, and his eyes shut. His young and fair features were almost as death-like as those of the form beside him, and almost as fixed; but *his* was the hush of exhausted anguish, and *hers* of perfect peace. Her brow smooth, her lids closed, her lips wearing the expression of a smile. No angel in heaven could be more beautiful than she appeared; and I partook of the infinite calm in which she lay. My mind was never in a holier frame, than while I gazed on that untroubled image of Divine rest. I instinctively echoed the words she had uttered, a few hours before. 'Incomparably beyond and above us all! Whether still on earth or now in heaven, her spirit is at home with God!

This passage, with its extraordinarily excised account of childbirth from the novel's surrogate mother is revealing of deeply embedded assumptions about how women are and have been viewed. Childbirth, as an experience belonging to the private sphere of womanhood, has traditionally been marginalised in literature. The

 CHECK THE BOOK

New French Feminisms edited by Marks and de Courtivron (1981) offers a compelling collection of essays which look at the different ways in which 'woman' can be read.

CHECK THE BOOK

Julia Kristeva's essay *Stabat Mater*, in the same volume as Cixous' essay, is also illuminating in theorising the conflicting discourses of maternity.

contemporary **feminist** critic Helene Cixous (1980) famously announced in her essay 'The Laugh of the Medusa', 'For if there's one thing that's been repressed, here's just the place to find it: in the taboo of the pregnant woman.'

Here Brontë subordinates the account of childbirth as a central and life-changing event in women's lives to the ideological view of women as the 'angel in the house'. Clearly the birth of Cathy is a life-changing event for Catherine, indeed it is a life-threatening event for her, resulting in her death. A feminist reading of this passage might focus on an investigation of the impact upon identity for a woman carrying and then giving birth to a child. The bodily experience of giving birth inevitably raises questions of self and other. Being pregnant challenges our usual notions of identity and individuality: two individuals are in one body, which must then divide into two to produce the iconic figure of mother and child.

Brontë highlights the complex integration of the duality by naming both individuals Catherine. The maternal self articulates something about identity which is inadmissible to the nineteenth-century novel except in the ambiguous, repetitive and doubling terms in which Brontë bravely chooses to write. Maternity radically challenges conventional ideas of where and when an individual begins and ends.

For Julia Kristeva, the maternal condition, the other inside the self, provides a radical challenge to concepts of identity and difference that underlie our whole signifying system.

The confusion of identities threatens to collapse a signifying system based on the paternal law of differentiation. It would seem that the concept of motherhood automatically throws into question ideas concerning the self, boundaries between self and other, and hence identity.

Nelly Dean, the novel's nurturing, surrogate mother, who brings the narrative into being, has her own story subdued by those of her 'nurslings', and also here submits to the authoritative discourses of religion and law to filter her understanding of the meaning of this event for Catherine.

PART THREE

CRITICAL APPROACHES

As has already been noted, *Wuthering Heights* is a novel that has given rise to a bewildering array of critical responses. J. Hillis Miller usefully catalogues the variety of interpretations at hand:

> There have been interpretations of *Wuthering Heights* in terms of the fair-haired girl and the dark-haired boy ...; or ... the symmetry of the family relations in the novel, or ... the laws of private property in Yorkshire; or ... in ... Freudian terms as a thinly disguised sexual drama ...; or as ... a conflict between two cosmological forces, calm and storm ...; or as a moral tale of the futility of grand passion ... or as the expression of a multitude of incompatible partial selves breaking down the concept of a unitary self ..., or in ... Marxist terms.   (1982, p. 50)

GENRE

Plot summaries are never sufficiently revealing of the text's effects, which is why the manner of telling the story is as important as the story itself, and also why it is worth paying the same generosity of attention to form as to content. *Wuthering Heights* has famously been considered a generically puzzling book to categorise. With its confident originality it appears to belong to the tradition of the *roman personnel* (the lived fiction). The relationship between art and life provides the central quest for biographer-critics. For example, Brontë's first biographer-critic, A. Mary F. Robinson (1883, p. 217) painstakingly traced aspects of Heathcliff's behaviour to aspects of Branwell Brontë, Emily's brother. Biographer-critics saw the task of literary criticism being that of exploring the relationships between fiction and reality. In fact Charlotte Brontë's responses to some of the early criticisms of *Wuthering Heights* seems to endorse this kind of critical approach.

> **CONTEXT**
>
> Biographer-critics of the nineteenth century considered the novel as if the key to understanding it lay in drawing parallels between Brontë's life and that of her characters.

Other attempts to categorise the novel have seen it as a **Gothic novel** preoccupied with the fantastic and supernatural; a fairy tale 'in which there is no semblance of reason'; a negotiation of the

QUESTION

To what extent is
this novel a good
example of the
Gothic Romance?

nineteenth century **novel of manners**, looking at the relationships
between culture and nature; a **romantic** novel, given its pervading
fascination with dreams and the unconscious, and the status it
accords the imagination; and a visionary novel, preoccupied with
metaphysical issues of mystical politics, witness the contrast
Brontë draws between conventional religion and the overarching
metaphysical truths of love and unconventional perception. This
focus on genres is not without its implications for our reading of
the text, or its characters.

Nancy Armstrong (in Stoneman, 1993), for example, argues that the
'enigmatic' figure of Heathcliff is the result of his crossing between
literary genres – the romantic genres of the early nineteenth century,
and early Victorian domestic realism.

CHARACTERISATION

Of all forms of literature novels are particularly compelling because
they seduce us into believing that in reading we are actually
expanding our knowledge of people and life. Of course, readers
know that characters are not real people, yet it is difficult to follow
any novel if one constantly reminds oneself that the characters are
merely literary constucts. Indeed one of the primary ways in which
we might judge a novel is whether or not we care sufficiently for its
characters. In *Wuthering Heights* Brontë offers us an intriguing
array of characters and narrators. There are two principal narrators
in this novel, which throws into question the authority of the
narrator. The aim of the classical narrator, as Frederic Jameson has
noted in *The Political Unconscious* (1981) is:

> to restore the coordinates of a face-to-face storytelling
> institution which has been effectively disintegrated by the
> printed book and even more definitively by the commodification
> of literature and culture.   (p. 155)

That is to say, the conventional narrator confers upon the novel
something of the authenticity of a spoken narrative. The presence of
the narrator is comforting, since the narrator is by virtue of his or

her role, a survivor: the narrator must survive to tell the retrospective tale. The narrator has an authority, which is made even more dramatic in nineteenth-century fiction on account of the fact that nearly all narrators are male. It is doubly significant therefore that Brontë chooses two narrators, one male and one female, and that the narrative of Nelly Dean outranks and dispossesses that of Lockwood, the male narrator.

The construction of two narrators, neither of which are seen to be entirely reliable or impartial, formulates for the reader a means of reading what the **post-structuralist** critic Pierre Macherey has called the 'not-said'. Able to read 'between the lines' of Nelly and Lockwood's narratives, the reader is able to interpret information from the text which is never made explicit. In distinguishing between 'reliable' and 'unreliable' accounts, therefore the reader is able to construct a body of knowledge from which to make judgements about the text, and its characters. As Catherine Belsey points out in *Critical Practice* (1980):

> In *Wuthering Heights* the inadequacies of the perceptions of
> Lockwood or Nellie (sic) Dean do not prevent the reader from
> seeming to apprehend the real nature of the relationship between
> Catherine and Heathcliff.   (p. 78)

The fact that we can perceive the accounts given by the narrators as partisan and informed by ideology permits us to read what the narrators literally *cannot* tell us.

Equally tantalisingly, Brontë plays with our expectations of characters as discrete and coherent individuals. They extend their influence beyond the grave; they share each other's names and moods and they exemplify all manner of contradictions.

It is conventional to consider characterisation in terms of identity: what characterises this person? how are they identified? One of the key elements of identity might be thought to be the name, yet *Wuthering Heights* is a novel in which there scarcely seem sufficient names to go round. There is a constant doubling of names which repetitiously trace each other through the three generations of the

QUESTION

Compare the roles of the two narrators and consider the implications of Brontë's decision to employ such a device.

novel. This section will consider the characterisation of the major characters of the novel.

CATHERINE

The reader's first introduction to Catherine Earnshaw is an introduction to the signature of a ghost; her name is scratched upon the window-ledge in her childhood bedroom, the room where Lockwood will have his disturbing nightmares. We cannot avoid the figure of Catherine, it is carved into the very text. At the end of the novel, Heathcliff is tormented by everything which signals to him his loss of Catherine, she is as elusive and forbidden to him as she is incomprehensible to Lockwood. Thus the characterisation of Catherine starts and ends in an enigma: the world of the novel is testament to her character, but it is testament to a character that can leave only the ghostly signs of itself behind.

The names which Lockwood finds inscribed upon the window – Catherine Earnshaw, Catherine Linton, Catherine Heathcliff – can be read as indicative of Catherine's fractured or fragmented social identity. Catherine struggles with conflicting options for selfhood as she tries to combine two irreconcilable lives: the life of passion fully experienced, and the life of social convention that secures her to either her father or her husband. Her assertion to Nelly Dean 'I *am* Heathcliff' (Vol. 1, Ch. 9, p. 87) is both dramatic and memorable, but it cannot stabilise her identity since Heathcliff too is enigmatic and uncertain.

QUESTION

With reference to two of the following sets of oppositions consider their function for the production of meaning in this novel:

- nature/culture
- duty/desire
- male/female
- spirituality/ materialism.

The conflict that disturbs Catherine's sense of self is played out in the novel through the themes of culture versus nature. In deciding to marry Edgar Linton, Catherine chooses culture over nature. This is directly contrasted with a narrative insistence upon her love of nature and her oneness with nature. As a child, for example, rather than read, she and Heathcliff prefer to scramble on the moors. Her diary, however, which documents the fact, pays scrupulous attention to her jettisoning of the book, but neglects to describe her impression of the moors. From Catherine's perspective nature does not need to be named, and it does not lend itself to narrative representation or culture. If we accept this reading, then

Catherine's choice of Edgar over Heathcliff cannot be expected to be successful.

It is, however, in character, for Nelly Dean's first introduction of Catherine is as 'mischievous and wayward' (Vol. 1, Ch. 4, p. 38), thus we can expect her to make unpredictable and surprising choices. Capable of great love and fidelity, Catherine is nevertheless equally capable of ruthless destruction, even if that entails her death and wretched misery for those she loves.

HEATHCLIFF

Heathcliff is described by Catherine as an 'unreclaimed creature' (Vol. 1, Ch. 10, p. 101). His mysterious capacity for self-invention, which defies the conventional categories of characterisation in the novel, renders him profoundly difficult to read for most of the other characters.

Unlike every other character in the novel, Heathcliff has only the singular name, which serves him as both Christian and surname. This places him radically outside social patterns and conventions. Heathcliff belongs first nowhere and finally anywhere. The fact that he inherits his name from a dead son also signals the potential for freeplay and invention, since this name might then be thought of as that of a ghost: a character who is no longer present.

Critics have most often cited Heathcliff as a **Byronic hero**: powerful, attractive, melancholy and brutal. Through most of the first volume of the novel Heathcliff's rise to power details the ascension of the **romantic** hero, with his intrusion into and transformation of a conventional and socially limited world. However, by making such romantic conventions manifest in an energetic new form, Heathcliff actually cancels out romantic possibilities and reduces that system to mere superstition. Thus in creating Heathcliff, Brontë may well have been acknowledging Byron's influence. But in the character of Catherine she also suggests a revision of Byron and demonstrates his vision as a fundamentally male literary myth.

CHECK THE BOOK

An early description of a mysterious brooding male can be found in Emily Brontë's 1839 poem 'The soft unclouded blue of air'. *Complete Poems: Emily Brontë* (1995).

CHECK THE NET
Refer to Clifton Snider's online text on vampires and *Wuthering Heights* for some excellent examples.

As a foundling, Heathcliff is introduced into the close-knit family structure as an outsider; he is perceived as both gift and threat and these contesting identifications form part of the compelling undecidability of his character. Contradiction typifies Heathcliff. To Catherine he is brother and lover; to Isabella he is romantic hero and pitiless oppressor; he epitomises potency, yet he fathers an exceptionally frail child. He encompasses vast philosophical opposites: love and death, culture and nature, evil and heroism. Some critics, most notably Clifton Snider, have focused on the supernatural qualities of this novel to read Heathcliff as vampiric. Certainly there is evidence of his bloodthirstiness, and Snider carefully marshals it all, but whether we read Heathcliff as monstrous or Byronic hero, he disturbs the conventional structure of the novel, and of the world created within it.

EDGAR

Edgar represents the world of conventional morality to which Heathcliff is the antithesis. Edgar's world is an interior world, and we first peep in on him as a child, poetically pictured by Heathcliff for Nelly Dean. Edgar's interior is:

> a splendid place, carpeted with crimson, and crimson-covered chairs and tables, and a pure white ceiling bordered by gold, a shower of golden glass-drops hanging in silver chains from the centre and shimmering with little soft tapers.
>
> (Vol. 1, Ch. 6, p. 48)

In the midst of this sumptuous environment, the description of which sits so uncomfortably in Heathcliff's mouth, stands Edgar, weeping by the fire. And Heathcliff despises him for his pettiness.

The descriptions of Edgar as 'a doll', a 'spoiled child', a 'soft thing' and 'a lamb [who] threatens like a bull' (Vol. 1, Ch. 12, p. 113) establish Edgar as artificial in contrast to the elemental descriptions afforded to Heathcliff and Catherine. And yet although there is no way that Edgar can satisfy Catherine, he nevertheless loves her in a conventional way as his wife, and when she is ill, he tends her devotedly.

It is rather a commonplace of criticism to read Edgar as effeminate, in contrast to the savage masculinity of Heathcliff. The **feminist** critics Gilbert and Gubar (1979) have reversed this trend, reading Edgar as masculine and Heathcliff as feminine. Edgar's masculinity, they argue, is that of social power. He legitimately inherits Thrushcross Grange; his books and his library establish him as a man of letters and therefore of influence. Nelly's constant reference to Edgar as 'the master' reveals her opinion of him as someone with social power. Heathcliff on the other hand is a cuckoo with no established parentage or inheritance. His lack of formal education places him in an inferior social position.

Edgar Linton is described as lacking spirit, and this can be read in two ways. Conventionally, he does lack the vigour that characterises Catherine and Heathcliff. However, he also lacks their ghostliness, the spectral quality which sets them apart and lends them mystery. By comparison Edgar's corporeality is easy to read. He is not troubled by internal contradiction, and he remains in his place throughout the novel, living at Thrushcross Grange as boy and man, and finally resting in his grave alongside the body of his wife.

ISABELLA

As Edgar's sister, Isabella's characterisation is closely associated with his. Indeed she is only ever seen in relation to other characters. Isabella's infatuation for Heathcliff, which structurally parallels Edgar's fascination with Catherine, fails to develop into a mature and unselfish love. Isabella's infatuation with Heathcliff is as a direct result of her cultural life: she can only read Heathcliff as a **romantic** hero and she never entirely abandons her fantasy of Heathcliff as the Byronic lover even when it is clear that his spontaneous love of Catherine has transformed itself into a determined lust for revenge, for which Isabella is only a cipher or vehicle. Feminist critics, looking at the novel from the perspective of **gynocriticism** have devoted their attention to the brutal realities of Isabella's position as a battered wife, and have theorised the power relations that seem to make her complicit in her oppression.

 CHECK THE BOOK

See Mills et al., *Feminist Readings, Feminists Reading* (1989) for a provocative and wide-ranging collection of essays from a number of feminist positions.

 QUESTION

Is Isabella a victim of the genre of Romance?

CONTEXT

It is possible, following Gilbert and Gubar (1979), to read Linton as an example of the gender-ambiguity with which Brontë imbues her characters. Linton displays many of the characteristics that a Victorian readership would be used to associating with typically female characters: he is manipulative, fickle, sickly, babyish – 'sucking a stick of sugar candy' (Vol. 2, Ch. 14, p. 276) and enfeebled in his relationship to dominant characters.

LINTON

Linton Heathcliff is a contradiction in terms. His name signifies the unnatural union between Heathcliff and the Lintons or between passion and convention and his sickly nature demonstrates the impossibility of such a union. In Linton both love and convention emerge as corrupted by each other. Brontë reserves for Linton her most scathing imagery: he is described as: 'a pet', a 'puling chicken' and a 'whelp' (Vol. 2, Ch. 5, pp. 199, 205, 206).

Like both his parents, however, Linton's view of the world is singular, and it is his inability to see it in any but his own terms which renders him absolutely available for manipulation by Heathcliff.

HARETON

Of his generation Hareton's character is perhaps the most intriguing, reversing the comparative lack of interest we feel for his father, Hindley. Hareton is brutalised by Heathcliff, structurally repeating Heathcliff's own suffering at the hands Hindley.

Hareton's relationship with Cathy has similarly been read as mirroring Heathcliff's with Catherine, in as much as he is desirous of impressing her, and he is proud in her presence. His love of Cathy however, might be said more closely to resemble Edgar's love of Catherine, in as much as it is moderate yet tender, devoted yet restrained. Hareton also exhibits an unwavering love for Heathcliff, in spite of the ill-treatment he has received at his hands. Like Catherine, Hareton is constant in his initial affections, and when Heathcliff first arrives into his life they form an alliance against Hindley.

Although Hareton's name is inscribed above the door of *Wuthering Heights*, his inability to read, coupled with the repetitious doubling of names and signatures, means that he fails to inherit his rightful property. The structural doubling of names means that there is no guarantee of inheritance. Inheritance requires a stable system of patriarchal legitimacy and uncontested identity. Hareton is dispossessed by Heathcliff, but can also be seen as a rewriting of

Heathcliff, a surrogate or symbolic Heathcliff. He is finally able to repossess the Heights only to be immediately assimilated into the cultural **hegemony** of the Grange.

The development of Hareton's characterisation revolves around his education. He is initially nursed by Nelly, the novel's surrogate mother, and under her tuition he begins to learn his letters. However, left to the ministrations of his dissolute and unpredictable father, Hindley, Hareton grows wild and uncultivated, unable to read, and with no social skills. His attempts at self-improvement are the source of mockery and derision by Linton and Cathy, and it is not until the end of the novel that he is able to acquire the skills necessary for him to achieve social status with Cathy and come into his rightful inheritance. The description of him being taught these skills is not without some diminution of his sexual potency, as he sits meekly to be alternately kissed or chastised as he learns. The domestic romance which typifies the final union between Cathy and Hareton may well resolve some of the conflicts that thwart the other relationships in the novel, but their union lacks the grand passion, the wild power of the original love between Catherine and Heathcliff.

QUESTION

Is *Wuthering Heights* a convincing domestic romance? Consider with reference to the character of Hareton Earnshaw.

CATHY

Structurally the second Cathy can be seen as revising her mother's story. She achieves her identity at the price of her mother's, and Edgar always differentiates her in relation to the first Catherine, whose name he never diminished. Unlike Linton, who has the misfortune of inheriting the worst of both his parents, Cathy appears to have inherited the good from both hers. She is described by Nelly as:

> the most winning thing that ever brought sunshine into a desolate house – a real beauty in face – with the Earnshaws' handsome dark eyes, but the Lintons' fair skin and small features, and yellow curling hair. Her spirit was high, though not rough, and qualified by a heart, sensitive and lively to excess in its affections. That capacity for fierce attachments reminded me of her mother; still she did not resemble her; for she could be soft and mild as a dove, and she had a gentle voice, and a pensive

expression: her anger was never furious; her love never fierce; it
was deep and tender.   (Vol. 2, Ch. 4, p. 187)

This character reference from Nelly is not inconsiderable, and it
influences the way we reflect upon the sour behaviour of Cathy
Heathcliff as she comports herself in the first volume of the novel.
However, it must be recalled that Nelly is here speaking to
Lockwood, whom she sees as a possible escape route for Cathy,
should he be induced to fall in love with her. Brontë also qualifies
Nelly's reference with her descriptions of Cathy's early relationship
with Hareton.

We are privy to reports of Cathy's pride, and her insensitive
mockery of Hareton's lack of formal knowledge. The resolution of
the novel in which she and Hareton form their attachment is
something of a mythical resolution, a **romantic** conclusion which
transcends the central conflicts of the novel to restore a traditional
novelistic plot of courtship and marriage. Cathy and Hareton's
relationship restores to the novel a version of domestic bliss that
was the Victorian ideal, but it is well to bear in mind that Brontë's is
a version in which Cathy clearly has the upper hand.

NELLY

QUESTION

'It is possible, from
a feminist
perspective, to
read the figure of
Nelly Dean as
representing the
position of the
woman writer in
nineteenth-
century England.'
Discuss.

Nelly Dean is the second and the dominant narratorial voice in this
novel. She takes up the story from Lockwood and gives it both
substance and credence. Lockwood's inability to read the signs of
the culture in which he finds himself cannot sustain the story,
though it acts to remind us that all narratorial voices, including
Nelly's, are partial.

Nelly Dean is a local, and has known each generation of the
Earnshaw and Linton families. She is therefore well-placed to offer
Lockwood a commentary upon the events she describes. Her
position of servant is differentiated from that of the other servants,
both in terms of the fact that she appears to move effortlessly
between the two houses, mediating between their differences, and in
terms of her voice. Nelly Dean does not share a regional dialect
with the other servants, although she understands it perfectly well.
She also emerges as an educated woman, having read most of the

books in the library at Thrushcross Grange – the house of culture – and in having experienced the vicissitudes of life at Wuthering Heights – the house of nature.

In keeping with her dual roles, Nelly has two names, Ellen, her given name, which is used by those wishing to accord her respect, and Nelly – the name her peers and familiars employ.

QUESTION

Consider the importance of names in this novel.

Nelly Dean is one of the most interesting characters of the novel not least because of the language she uses. Both feminist and Marxist critics have acknowledged that in looking at literary texts it is important to consider the way in which women's access to language and education is ideologically determined. Nelly Dean, however, occupies a unique cultural position in this novel. She has access to a range of discourses that might be considered beyond her ken in terms of her position as a family servant; yet as the central narrator Brontë presents her as a speaking subject, partially excluded from culture but nonetheless positioned so as to be able to comment upon it. Nelly acts as a surrogate mother to many of the motherless characters in this novel: she brings up Hareton for the first five years of his life; she cares for Cathy from birth through to her marriage to Linton; she regrets the brevity of her charge of Linton Heathcliff, which is forced by circumstance; and she acts as confidant and adviser to Catherine and Heathcliff. She also acts as a mother-figure to Lockwood as she nurses him back to health. As surrogate mother Nelly provides food and moral sustenance to her nurslings. Q.D. Leavis, writing in the 1930s, has this to say of Nelly Dean: 'Nelly Dean is most carefully, consistently and convincingly created for us as the normal woman, whose truly feminine nature satisfies itself in nurturing all the children of the book in turn' (in Stoneman, 1993, p. 28).

Evidently, contemporary feminist critics might take issue with this conflation of essential feminine nature and maternity, but this was certainly the ideology of the day for Victorian readers.

This reading of Nelly as a mother-figure alerts us to another of her roles, for Nelly is a Mother Goose, the teller of this fairytale, the keeper of its wisdom. Marina Warner (1994) observes in her analysis of fairytales that: 'The goose was sacred to the Goddess of Love, Aphrodite' (p. 51). The name might also be a corruption of Mother Gossip. Both of these definitions are pertinent to the figure of Nelly, since the knowledge she conveys is at least twofold: it is about women's experience, and it is about the nature of love. The fact that Brontë chooses to tell this (fairy) story via a series of narratives deeply imbricated in the gossip of the hearth and heart of the family, carefully negotiates the audience's inclinations. Drawing its appeal from its oral traditions Nelly knows that her story has to entertain and ensnare us. Yet her voice is rooted in the realist narrative. With her love of a well-brushed hearth and gleaming copper pans, Nelly weaves for us a fairy tale of mythic proportions. Given our narrator's sympathies we are inevitably drawn to the novel's celebration of passion, and find the strictures of its dominant discourses of marriage and religion as stifling and incomprehensible as do its main protagonists.

RECURRING THEMES

LOVE

QUESTION

Is this novel the 'greatest of love stories' or an account of the impossibility of such a desire?

Wuthering Heights has been called the greatest of love stories, and the novel's attraction as a love story is not difficult to identify. Indeed, the love story is central to *Wuthering Heights*. It is a novel which explores love from a number of different perspectives: domestic, maternal, social, **romantic**, religious and **transcendent**. But it is also a novel which explores that theme through a range of conventions which startled and confused its contemporary readership and still causes us to reflect on our conventional notions of what constitutes the genre of the love story. In the central relationship between Catherine and Heathcliff, Brontë takes the sweep of idealised romance for example and fuses it with gothic fantasy and horror. In the comfortable domestic realism of Catherine's marriage to Edgar, Brontë interleaves a discourse of illness and childbirth which eventually leads to death.

Narcissism characterises the relationship between Isabella and Heathcliff, and similarly that between Catherine and Edgar. When Heathcliff's love of Catherine corrupts into a lust for revenge, his passion transgresses powerful social taboos: he lies with her dead body in the grave; he tyrannises his dying son in order to accumulate wealth; and he abuses his wife gratuitously and without compunction. Catherine, unable to reconcile her passion for Heathcliff with her marriage to Edgar resorts to self-destruction: 'I'll try to break their hearts by breaking my own' (Vol. 1, Ch. 11, p. 116). She refuses food, wilfully exposes herself to a chill when she is feverish and works herself up into a nervous agitation while she is carrying Edgar's child. She dies in childbirth, and her daughter is born two months premature. The greatest of love stories, then, is explored through the profoundest acts of violence. Jay Clayton's (1987) analysis of the love between Catherine and Heathcliff reads it as necessarily deferred. The only way to posit the possibility of a realm of absolute love is to point to it as the lost object of desire. He says: 'Catherine's declaration of love attempts to recover a lost state of being even as it claims that this lost unity will endure forever … Catherine and Heathcliff's tragic tale depends on their being separated' (p. 82).

The love story then is one that is always and already constructed about a loss.

NATURE AND CULTURE

The dichotomy between nature and culture, which forms part of the thematic structure of this novel, is played out in the relationship between the two houses: Wuthering Heights, which represents nature and Thrushcross Grange representing culture. The theme is developed in the ways in which the houses similarly represent enclosure or exposure. The opposition between these two displays them as both antagonistic and subtly matched. This is a conflict that can be interpreted in a number of ways: in historical terms as a rural way of life contends against industrialisation; in psychological terms as a struggle between the ego and the id; in sexual terms as a choice between experience and representation.

QUESTION

Consider the importance of the opposition between nature and culture in this novel.

The representations of nature in this novel are almost invariably brutal or hostile. From the very beginning Lockwood identifies himself as a man of culture, appropriately living at the Grange, and utterly incapable of reading the signs of nature. His abortive attempt to negotiate the snowstorm and read the human signs which underlie the elements are testimony to this.

Nature is neither legible, nor representable in this novel. Lockwood cannot read its signs, and Catherine refuses to name it. Nor is nature seen as unremittingly cruel in comparison to culture. The representations of culture see it as equally dangerous, and violent.

The novel opens with Lockwood's account of the countryside and his impression of his place within it:

> This is certainly a beautiful country. In all England, I do not believe that I could have fixed on a situation so completely removed from the stir of society. A perfect misanthropist's Heaven – and Mr Heathcliff and I are such a suitable pair to divide the desolation between us.   (Vol. 1, Ch. 1, p. 3)

 QUESTION

Consider the ways in which Brontë uses the landscape as a metaphor in this novel.

Lockwood inhabits the landscape of the moors as a tourist. As a tourist he is a consumer, converting the landscape and the lives of its occupants into a private aesthetic experience. He contributes nothing to its maintenance; he fails to understand its dangers or even to read its beauty except in a Romanticised and sentimental way. In Nancy Armstrong's essay 'Imperialist Nostalgia and *Wuthering Heights*' (1992) she argues that: 'Lockwood's journey into the wastelands, farms and villages is a journey back in time. As the story regresses through preceding generations of the Earnshaw family, it appears to be taking us back to the primitive beginnings of the culture' (p. 435).

In *Wuthering Heights,* Brontë employs landscape imagery in particular to represent heightened emotional states that would otherwise defy representation in the nineteenth-century novel. Even though the emotions were couched in more or less poetic language, this novel caused such a public outcry upon publication that Charlotte Brontë was required to defend it. Her defence consisted of situating her sister precisely in the nostalgic rural environment that cannot be held responsible for its actions.

> To identify the author with the region that she represented, Charlotte infused her with nostalgia. She reframed the novel …

as something 'rustic all through. It is moorish and wild, and knotty as the root of heath,' Charlotte's preface arrogated these same qualities to the author as well, 'nor was it natural that it should be otherwise, the author being herself a native and nursling of the moors.' (p. 449)

This relationship between landscape and the emotions can be read in both directions. Margaret Homans in her essay 'Repression and Sublimation of Nature in *Wuthering Heights*' (1978) takes up a point first made by Leo Bersani about the destructiveness of nature. Pointing out that nature is hardly ever directly represented in this novel which appears to be about nature, Homans argues that Emily Brontë chooses indirect methods such as metaphor or anecdote as a mode of repressing its more threatening aspects.

MORALITY

There are at least three views of morality which are pitted against each other in this novel. Conventional, institutionalised morality might be said to be most forcibly represented by Joseph, and it is represented as pious, restrictive, domineering and legislative. Ever ready with a Biblical quotation or religious homily, Joseph provides a relentlessly sour commentary upon the activities of the other members of the Heights household. His is the restrictive voice of social convention which intrudes upon this house of nature, regulating it and judging it.

The second form of morality which is explored in the novel focuses attention upon the morality of authenticity, of being true to the self. In the light of this morality, Catherine's marriage to Edgar is judged as an extreme act of bad faith which precipitates all subsequent tragedy and evil.

The third form of morality which is explored is that of self-interest over altruism. Many of the characters in the novel appear to act for the good of others, and yet their actions serve the aggrandisement of their own power or knowledge. For example, Nelly Dean withholds or reveals her knowledge apparently arbitrarily, but her choices to do so invariably influence the events of the novel. Examples of this are when she neglects to tell Edgar about Catherine's illness and

CHECK THE BOOK
Writing Worlds: Discourse, Text and Metaphor in the Representation of Landscape, edited by Trevor J. Barnes and James. S. Duncan (1992) offers a range of insightful essays focusing on the representations of landscape within a variety of texts.

when she informs him of Cathy's correspondence with Linton. On each occasion her decision has profound consequences for the events of the novel.

EDUCATION

Brontë seems ambivalent about the effects of education. The denial of education to Heathcliff is perceived as a form of social punishment and humiliation. It robs Heathcliff of status both within the family and within society. Yet Hareton's painful acquisition of a formal education in the final part of the novel can be read as having both beneficial and negative implications. Hareton acquires the learning and social skills required for union with Cathy; but he also appears to lose power – including sexual power – in his submission to this option. This might be read in terms of a repetition of Catherine's choice earlier in the text, where she trades authentic selfhood for social privilege.

Lockwood prides himself on his educational standing, but repeatedly misreads both his environment and his companions. Education in the form of reading, however, dignifies Nelly Dean in her role as narrator and lends her social status.

Brontë appears to make a distinction between education and intelligence, and prizes intelligence both in terms of information and in terms of emotional wisdom far above education.

IMAGERY AND SYMBOLISM

BOUNDARIES

A number of critics have commented on the novel's emphasis upon physical boundaries like walls, windows, locks, gates and doorways. Throughout the novel these boundaries are both defended and breached. Lockwood is barred from the Heights when he first visits; he then attempts to bar Cathy's ghost; Catherine and Heathcliff are barred from Thrushcross Grange; Each character seeks control by locking others in or out, each episode details some imprisonment or exclusion. Overall, however, the novel documents the futility of every such attempt.

Dorothy Van Ghent has famously argued that the various windows and barriers serve both to separate and connect polar opposites: inside and outside; human and ghost. However, all the enclosures are violated. No boundary remains intact, neither property, nor bedroom, nor body, nor book, nor grave, nor dream. The contradictions exist in a tension which is both compelling and fragile, threatening and vulnerable.

TEXTUALITY

This is a novel which abounds with texts, from Catherine's diaries, to Joseph's biblical quotations, from the books in the Thrushcross Grange library which keep Edgar occupied while Catherine is dying to the books which Hareton hurls into the fire in his public humiliation. Letters too form a crucial part of the action of the novel, pushing events forward and aiding character development.

Our first introduction to Wuthering Heights as a building is via the inscription that sits above the door. This inscription which reads 1500 and Hareton Earnshaw is one which, both in terms of its numbers and its letters, bears only a puzzling relationship to the house's history but in fact attests to the house as a House, a structure of kinship and inherited power. Within the novel each text might be seen to represent the heterogeneity of the whole, for none of the various texts correspond with each other: even the letters which pass between the various characters fail to communicate. Each text stands as a testimony to contradiction, to supplementarity, to the impossibility of uncontestable readings.

 CHECK THE BOOK
For an interesting structuralist analysis of language and textuality have a look at the work of the French critic Roland Barthes, in particular *Image Music Text* (1977).

As J. Hillis Miller has observed, the novel comes to the reader packaged in text, in terms of its innumerable prefaces and introductions. Such presentation is now so standard that it is difficult to negotiate the end of one text and the beginning of the next, or the novel proper.

Wuthering Heights is a novel which is rich in **semiotics**. It abounds with a superabundance of signs, from the gravestones (standing as a sign of absence) to the memoranda of Catherine that Heathcliff sees in everything around him.

Letters and the epistolary form, were often used in nineteenth-century literature, and served a number of purposes. One of the functions of letters is that they allow certain facts and characters' opinions to be expressed even in their absence. In this novel, in which the letters rarely reach their intended recipients and are largely incomprehensible when they do, they even more obviously point to absence, to the impossibility of fulfilment. That this is the case is established at the very beginning of the novel when Lockwood notes the date and name above the main door of Wuthering Heights, an inscription which we expect to indicate the nature of the house's history and ownership, but which seems entirely at odd with what is actually the case. The inadequacy of the many letters which are sent in this novel to represent the intentions of the sender is a fact attested to frequently. For example Isabella's uncommonly long letter to Nelly Dean commences:

> I came last night to Wuthering Heights and heard, for the first time, that Catherine has been, and is yet, very ill. I must not write to her I suppose and my brother is either too angry or too distressed to answer what I send him. Still, I must write to somebody and the only choice left me is you.
>
> (Vol. 1, Ch. 13, p. 134)

In this letter, Isabella urges Nelly not to respond to her in writing, but to 'call ... very soon'.

Like the diary entries and the dreams, this letter is one of a number of significant digressions from the main narrative progression of this novel, others of which include Catherine's diary, Zillah's narrative and Heathcliff's confessions to Nelly. *Wuthering Heights* is a self-consciously literary novel, almost obsessively concerned with reading and writing as a dramatic ploy for moving the action of the novel forward.

ANIMAL IMAGERY

Brontë frequently uses animal imagery as a metaphor for some human frailty or moral deficiency: Linton, for example is described as a 'chicken' (Vol. 2, Ch. 6, p. 205), Hareton a 'dog' (Vol. 2, Ch. 18, p. 307), Heathcliff a 'mad dog' (Vol. 2, Ch. 1, p. 160), 'savage beast'

CONTEXT

In the nineteenth century the confessional form of the letter, or the diary entry was understood to be a mode of exploring the unknown.

(Vol. 2, Ch. 2, p. 167). Lockwood's mistaken apprehension of a heap of dead rabbits for a chairful of cats not only identifies him as unobservant, but also someone who is incapable of reading animal imagery and, given the preponderance of such imagery in this novel, it is therefore entirely appropriate that his narratorial role is quickly taken over by Nelly Dean. The description of the male characters in this novel as beasts can be read as underscoring Catherine as a reluctant bride. The fairytale structure of tales like Beauty and the Beast, Bluebeard, or Rumpelstiltskin permitted women writers to elaborate ideas about choice and love and popular romance within the historical and social context of the marriage contract in the nineteenth century.

As Mark Schorer (1949) points out, most of the animals in *Wuthering Heights* are wild: 'Hareton's whiskers encroached *bearishly* over his cheeks', and Heathcliff denies the paternity of 'that bear'... Heathcliff is a 'fierce, pitiless, *wolfish* man' (p. 547).

For the *Christian Remembrancer* in 1857, the recognition that Emily Brontë's 'heroine's scratch and tear, and bite, and slap ... The men ... roll, and grapple, and struggle, and throttle and clutch and tear and trample' was clear evidence of her moral degradation.

Clifton Snider has given a comprehensive account of the animal imagery in this novel, reading such imagery in terms of vampiric archetypes. He points out that this is a novel rife with vicious animals: that it is the bite from the Thrushcross Grange guard-dog Skulker which presents the initial disruption in the childhood relationship between Catherine and Heathcliff, and that Heathcliff himself is described as both supernatural a 'demon' and animal a 'mad dog':

DREAMS AND THE SUPERNATURAL

Dreams are an important key to knowledge in this novel, and the dreamwork and hallucinatory elements of the text have anticipated twentieth-century **psychoanalytic criticism**

Dreams demonstrate a way of thinking through the forbidden. They are equipped with a magic all their own. In the novel, dreams are

CONTEXT

In her childhood,
Emily Brontë was
influenced by the
household
servants who
recounted
supernatural tales
set in Northern
England.

clearly of central importance and their relation to magic, to visions, to ghostly apparitions is never understated.

Lockwood's dream of the child Cathy begging to be let in is disturbing on two levels. It is grisly, and the gratuitous cruelty of him sawing her wrist against the broken glass is uncomfortable. But as Frank Kermode suggests, it is also disturbing because neither Lockwood nor Heathcliff really believe that it was a dream. It therefore doubly resists integration into the rational.

The extravagance of the ghostly, the supernatural and the unearthly in this novel is entirely devoted to the relationship between Catherine and Heathcliff, and to descriptions of them as individuals. This achieves its most profound exemplification when Catherine is dying, and Heathcliff is described by Nelly as a 'creature [not] of my own species' (Vol. 2, Ch. 1, p. 160), and then again towards the end of the novel when she wonders 'is he a ghoul or a vampire?' (Vol. 2, Ch. 20, p. 327). As Clifton Snider suggests, Brontë's decision to make Heathcliff her hero can be read as an intervention into the Victorian prejudice against outsiders, such as gypsies and beggars, as well as their fascination for and prejudice against the supernatural.

Frank Kermode (1975) considers the dreams of the novel in his analysis, paying particular attention to the 'vision' that Nelly has by the signpost of the child Hindley who 'turns into' Hareton who in turn 'turns into' Heathcliff. He argues that although not strictly a dream this has many similarities with a real dream in terms of its transformations and displacements. The confusion of generations, Hindley Hareton and Heathcliff mingling and merging qualifies our sense of their identities and the sense of all narrative explanations offered in the text. Because Brontë refuses to offer us any naturalistic explanation of Nelly's experience it joins the plethora of occult phenomena which are 'only indeterminately related to the natural narrative. And this serves to muddle routine single readings, to confound explanation and expectation, and to make necessary a full recognition of the intrinsic plurality of the text' (p. 129).

Kermode sees the function of the dreams and visions in the novel as being specifically to disturb any 'natural' unifying reading which aims to 'make sense' of the story.

LANDSCAPE IMAGERY

Many critics have paid attention to Brontë's use of landscape imagery, and the way in which landscape frequently functions as a metaphor for human behaviour or characteristics in this novel. Mark Schorer (1949) notes that 'Human conditions are like the activities of the landscape, where rains flood ... spirits are at high water mark ... illnesses are weathered' (p. 545).

Faces too are like landscapes, with countenances regularly clouding over and then brightening. Catherine experiences whole 'seasons of gloom', and 'her humour was a mere vane for constantly varying caprices' (Vol. 2, Ch. 1, p. 158).

LANGUAGE AND STYLE

DIALECT

Brontë's use of the Yorkshire dialect has generally been considered to be an accurate rendition of the accent. In the second edition of the novel, which was edited and amended by Charlotte Brontë, Charlotte modified the rendering of Joseph's dialect in order to make it more comprehensible. Over time, Charlotte's edition has fallen from favour and most modern editions now take the first edition as their starting point. However, this use of dialect possibly earned Brontë's novel some of its early censure, since the language and manners of the local characters were criticised for being rough and coarse. Phonetic renditions of dialect are a sensitive issue, since they make for uncomfortable reading and so frequently rob the character of the possibilities for empathetic reading. However, if we take Joseph as an example, his dialect does not serve to make him ridiculous, but rather contributes to our interpretation of his authentic character. We read Joseph as cantankerous, moralising, unyielding and inflexible. The phonetic rendition of his dialect exemplifies his resistance to change and his hostility to strangers. It

CHECK THE BOOK

Psychoanalytic theorists such as Jay Clayton (1987) have drawn on the Lacanian view of language as alienating and alienation as a crucial part of what it means to be human, to consider Brontë's use of dialect and language style in her novel.

literally makes him 'difficult to read' or to understand. It thus
underlines something in his character. Nelly Dean would
undoubtedly understand and use this dialect herself, but Brontë's
decision to render her speech in standard English serves to
emphasise the fact that she is flexible and capable of using and
understanding different discourses according to her audience. It also
suggests that Nelly can manipulate information according to her
interests. Thus we can see Brontë's deliberate choice of writing now
in dialect and now in 'heard English' as an expression of character
and identity.

POETIC LANGUAGE

The superabundance of metaphor and symbol and the lyricism of
the descriptive passages have earned this novel praise for its poetic
language:

**CHECK
THE BOOK**
Much of the most
potent imagery in
Wuthering Heights
is also to be found
in Brontë's poetry.
*Emily Brontë: The
Complete Poems,*
see particularly
p. 55.

> One time, however, we were near quarrelling. He said the
> pleasantest manner of spending a hot July day was lying from
> morning till evening on a bank of heath in the middle of the
> moors, with the bees humming dreamily about among the
> bloom, and the larks singing high up over head, and the blue sky,
> and bright sun shining steadily and cloudlessly. That was his
> most perfect idea of heaven's happiness – mine was rocking in a
> rustling green tree, with a west wind blowing, and bright, white
> clouds flitting rapidly above; and not only larks, but throstles,
> and blackbirds, and linnets, and cuckoos pouring out music on
> every side, and the moors seen at a distance, broken into cool,
> dusky dells; but close by great swells of long grass undulating in
> waves to the breeze; and the woods and sounding water, and the
> whole world awake and wild with joy. He wanted all to lie in an
> ecstasy of peace; I wanted all to sparkle, and dance in a glorious
> jubilee.   (Vol. 2, Ch. 10, p. 245)

Brontë's evident pleasure in the sensual life and the pleasure she
takes in language are given full latitude in such passages. Lord David
Cecil (1958) praises the rhythm of Brontë's prose as 'unfailingly
beautiful; a varied, natural, haunting cadence, now buoyantly lilting,
now surging like the sea' (p. 191). In fact there are numerous
correspondences in this novel with Brontë's poetry. Compare, for

example Heathcliff's tormented account of being unable to sleep for love of Catherine, and desire to be reunited with her dead body with the poem *Sleep brings no joy to me* (Emily Brontë, *The Complete Poems*, 1995, p. 55).

DUAL NARRATION

Brontë frames her narrative in terms of a dual narration, a technique that was virtually unprecedented when she wrote *Wuthering Heights*. Her first narrator Lockwood is demonstrably unreliable: he mistakes social relationships and radically misreads Heathcliff from the beginning. Although Nelly Dean's narrative is somewhat less subject to contradiction and denial, it is nevertheless evidently informed by her own partiality, and from time to time her ulterior motives. We are never under the illusion Nelly Dean's is a neutral or objective narrative. The novel explicitly resists such consolations and insists upon the responsibilities of all readers and storytellers. Some **feminist** analyses have focused on the fact that Nelly Dean's narrative superscribes that of Lockwood, and have seen this as Brontë making an intervention into the male supremacist bias of much Victorian literature. Others have read it as a destabilising of the conventional authority of the narrative voice. However we choose to read it, it is clear that there is a redistribution of power when Nelly takes up the narrative.

During the period of the 1950s a series of articles appeared in the journal *Nineteenth Century Fiction* which debated the exact role of the narrators. John K. Mathison (1956) argued that 'Nelly is an admirable woman whose point of view ... the reader must reject', thus forcing the reader 'into an active participation in the book' (p. 106).

CHECK THE NET

www. victorianresearch. org has a wide range of provocative essays and articles.

In his essay 'The narrators of *Wuthering Heights*', published in 1957, Carl Woodring argues that Nelly and Lockwood can be read as both narrators and actors in the plot. According to his reading, the narrators are not merely neutral commentators on the action, but active participants in it. This shift of emphasis is a significant one in that it relocates the critical enquiry, moving it from the aesthetic question of structure to the moral question of responsibility.

PART FOUR

CRITICAL HISTORY

RECEPTION AND EARLY REVIEWS

Early reviews of the novel praised it for its imaginative potency while criticising it for being strange and ambiguous. In a biographical notice attached to many modern versions of the novel, Charlotte Brontë complains that the novel did not receive sufficient merit in its initial reception. But *Wuthering Heights* did not go unrecognised by its early readers. Literary critics repeatedly acknowledged its originality, genius and imaginative power – if they also complained about its moral ambiguity.

Following Charlotte Brontë's clarification of the gender of Ellis Bell, Victorian readers began to place *Wuthering Heights* in the gothic category, a category of literature peculiarly associated with women. Dante Gabriel Rossetti, in 1854, describes *Wuthering Heights* as 'a fiend of a book, an incredible monster, combining all the stronger female tendencies from Mrs Browning to Mrs Brownrigg. The action is laid in Hell, – only it seems places and people have no English names there.'

CHECK THE BOOK

Patsy Stoneman (1993) offers an accessible and representative selection of early reviews of *Wuthering Heights*.

For theVictorians, *Wuthering Heights* was inarguably an immoral and uncivilised book. It deeply challenged all their ideas about propriety and literature. Equally by the 1920s, it was just as clear that its great value and message was metaphysical. Lord David Cecil, Professor of English Literature at Oxford, who helped to integrate *Wuthering Heights* into the canon of English Literature in his famous chapter in *Early Victorian Novelists* (1934). He argues that Brontë's motivation in *Wuthering Heights* was an exploration of the meaning of life: 'Her great characters exist in virtue of the reality of their attitude to the universe; they look before us on the simple epic outline which is all that we see of man when revealed against the huge landscape of the cosmic scene' (p. 151).

CRITICAL HISTORY

Wuthering Heights is a novel which has generated enormous critical attention. It is impossible here to give an account of everything that has been written and said about this novel. Doubtless, there are some important omissions but the review attempts to give a representative overview of some of the positions that it is possible to take up in relation to the text Charlotte Brontë's **romantic** explanation of Emily Brontë as an inspired genius has led many critics to search for the unconscious or hidden meaning of *Wuthering Heights*; it has influenced **psychoanalytic criticism** and certain kinds of **formalist** and **feminist** criticism.

Following Charlotte's lead, some nineteenth-century analyses of *Wuthering Heights* emphasised the psychological elements of the novel's plot and characters. The critic Sydney Dobell praised Emily Brontë for her portrayal of the 'deep unconscious' truth of Catherine Earnshaw's personality (in E. Jolly, ed., 1878, pp. 169–74). However, Dobell insisted that Wuthering Heights was an early work by Charlotte Brontë. According to Dobell, Brontë understood that 'certain crimes and sorrows are not so much the result of intrinsic evil as of a false position in the scheme of things'. Dobell's is a view that anticipates some **feminist** discussions of Catherine's choice.

Much early criticism tended to look to Brontë's life to understand elements in her work. For example, critics attempted to draw parallels between Brontë's depiction of Heathcliff and her brother Branwell. Such criticism is based on a view that the relationship between literature and the world is relatively straightforward, that reality exists and that it is literature's job to describe it. The role of literary criticism, according to this view, is to assess the accuracy of the representations, and also to assess the moral content of the work, for literature and the arts in general were held to be an integral part of the civilised life, and thus should contribute to the moral fabric of society.

QUESTION

Given the Victorian concept of literature as a morally edifying contributor to the civilised life, consider whether *Wuthering Heights* can be judged a work of inspired genius.

Not all early criticism, however, focused exclusively on the moral or biographical aspects of the text. Some early critics focused on the novel's relationship to other literary texts. A review in *The Examiner* in 1848 noted that Heathcliff was a **Byronic hero**. More sophisticated contemporary versions of this approach include Gilbert and Gubar's reading in *The Madwoman in the Attic* where they read the novel as a revision of the Miltonic myth of the Fall and Harold Bloom's reading of the novel as a critique of Byron's *Manfred*. Such readings see literature as part of the real life we lead, not just reflective of it, and argue that the literary texts we create respond to and modify those we have read.

Close attention to Brontë's novel begins with C.P. Sanger's *The Structure of Wuthering Heights* (1926) and Lord David Cecil's *Early Victorian Novelists* (1935) both of whom wished to distance criticism from moral judgement and proceed from an analysis of the formal elements of the text. Cecil's elaboration of the 'storm and calm' structure of *Wuthering Heights* has become one of the most widely accepted of all readings. He argues that the novel is based on a foundation of the dynamic relation between two spiritual principles:

**CHECK
THE NET**
For a comprehensive resource on Emily Brontë search **www. victorianweb.org**.

> the principle of storm – of the harsh, the ruthless, the wild, the dynamic; and …the principle of calm – of the gentle, the merciful, the passive and the tame … in spite of their apparent opposition these principles are not conflicting.
>
> (Cecil, 1958, p. 151)

In this critics such as Cecil and Sanger prepared the way for the **new critics** such as Mark Schorer. Schorer was the first to investigate patterns of imagery in *Wuthering Heights* in 1949. He sees the novel as a moral story about the futility of grand passion. Other new critics include Dorothy Van Ghent, who drew attention to the metaphors of windows and thresholds (see **Theme** on **boundaries**).

Contemporary criticism has tended to move on from such approaches. **Feminist** criticism has seen the novel in terms of its language, and in terms of the strategies and opportunities that are open to women in the novel. Feminist and gender criticism has also provided some interesting readings of the ambivalent representations of gender in *Wuthering Heights*, not the least of which is Gilbert and Gubar's reading of Heathcliff as 'female' in the sense that second sons, bastards and daughters are female. Heathcliff is 'female' because he is dispossessed of social power. He has no status, no social place and no property. He is only Heathcliff, never Mr Heathcliff, or the Master, in contrast to Edgar Linton. Heathcliff's rebellions against the social conventions of class, marriage and inheritance similarly suggest that he can be read as 'female' since endorsing such conventions only serves the interests of patriachial culture.

Marxist criticism has seen the novel in terms of its social relations, looking for the correspondences between the novel and the political, social and economic conditions under which it was produced. The first consistent attempt to read *Wuthering Heights* in terms of class oppression and struggle was David Wilson in 1947 in his article 'Emily Brontë: First of the Moderns':

> Distancing himself from the biographical theories of the novel's origins, Wilson dedicates his reading to the project of picturing 'Emily Brontë in a new light, the light of West Riding social history.   (p. 94)

CHECK THE BOOK

For a confirmation of this point see Juliet Barker's biography of the Brontës (1994).

He provides a detailed history of Haworth and its region, evidencing the freedom of its independent yeomen in medieval times from both the feudal system and from the Roman Church to claim a culture that was from very early on proudly politicised. He continues by describing how mechanised industry devastated local hand-loom weavers and gives detailed evidence that 'these social storms were far too near for the sisters to have lived the quiet secluded lives that have been pictured' (p. 96)

Wilson's purpose in such a reading is to account for the real social conditions in which a book like *Wuthering Heights* was produced, seeing it neither as the product of isolated genius nor as the muddled ramblings of a social recluse.

Arnold Kettle in *An Introduction to the English Novel* argues that the values represented in *Wuthering Heights*, against which

Heathcliff rebels, reflect the specific tyranny of Victorian capitalist society. Like Wilson, Kettle is keen to debunk the mystical aura surrounding Emily Brontë. He locates it as a story about real people living real lives with real concerns:

> *Wuthering Heights* is about England in 1847 ... [it] is concerned not with love in the abstract but with the passions of living people, with property-ownerships, ... the arrangement of marriages, the importance of education, the validity of religion, the relations of rich and poor.   (1981, p. 139)

QUESTION

With reference to either a Marxist or a Feminist perspective consider the ways in which Brontë subverts conventional power relationships.

Perhaps the most famous Marxist analysis of the novel is given by Terry Eagleton in *Myths of Power: A Marxist Study of the Brontës* (1975) in which he considers the novel in terms of its reference to class, economics and history. Where Wilson and Kettle tacitly rely on Marx's concept of literary representation being part of the cultural superstructure which relates directly to the economic base of society, Eagleton produces a structuralist development of marxist theory. Furthermore, Eagleton is interested in the novel's relationship to its culture's **ideology**, looking at how that ideology is both reflected and produced by the novel.

Because Marxists see ideology as what makes people choose to cooperate with, endorse and naturalise the class structure, they are particularly interested in the contradictions which arise at boundaries between classes and other social groups, contradictions which reveal ideology for what it is and not as the 'natural order' of things, or inevitable.

Eagleton gives us an orthodox marxist reading of Heathcliff's life as 'an extreme parody of capitalist activity' mimicking an ideology of self-help, enterprise and industry. However, his reading is not simply orthodox, since he refuses to jettison the bits of the novel that do not fit his reading. It is here, in the contradictions and slippages that, following the theoretical insights of Pierre Macherey, Eagleton finds the text's ideological resistance.

Eagleton argues that although it is possible to read Heathcliff as participating in an economic structure, he can also, because of his

unknown origins, be read as: 'a purely atomised individual …
outside the family and society in an opposing realm which can be
adequately imaged only as Nature.' The novel thus offers a
dialectical vision in which two contradictory versions of reality are
held in suspension. For Eagleton, the fascination of Heathcliff is
that he appears to have no place within society; he thus throws into
question all kinds of ideological assumptions and also highlights
Catherine's obvious rootlessness:

> Catherine, who does not expect to inherit, responds
> spontaneously to Heathcliff's presence; and because this
> antagonises Hindley she becomes after Earnshaw's death, a
> spiritual orphan as Heathcliff is a literal one. Both … become the
> 'outside' of the domestic structure.   (p. 103)

Eagleton, despite his impeccably marxist analysis, which considers
the processes and systems of domination and oppression within the
novel, has been criticised for the fact that his reading still takes
Heathcliff as the novel's central character. He was famously taken to
task for this by the Marxist-Feminist Literature Collective in 1977.
The Collective argued that a marxist analysis alone could not account
for the oppression of women. While marxism argues that all social
structures are determined by the relations of production, feminism
argues that the family constitutes a separate power-structure in which
women are further oppressed in the relations of *re*production.

 CHECK THE FILM
There have been
many film versions
of the book, the
earliest of which
was A.V. Bramble's
1920 silent film.

Two years before Eagleton's *Myths of Power*, in 1973, the Marxist
critic Raymond Williams had published an insightful reading of
Wuthering Heights in his book *The Country and the City*,
accounting for the relationship between Catherine and Heathcliff in
terms of alienation rather than oppression. Although he
acknowledges that it is class and property that divide Heathcliff and
Catherine he argues that the solution to their division is never
conceived of in terms of social reform. What Brontë privileges
above all, he argues, is human intensity and a profound connection
between people:

> The tragic separation between human intensity and any available
> social settlement is accepted from the beginning in the whole

design and idiom of the novel. The ... plot is ... sustained by a
single feeling, which is the act of transcendence.   (p. 176)

This concept of transcendence as a response to alienation from
social possibilities is also important in Eagleton's reading.

In the same year as *Myths of Power*, David Musselwhite published
an essay on *Wuthering Heights* in the Marxist Literary Journal *Red
Letters*, based on Louis Althusser's theory of ideology, elaborated in
response to Pierre Macherey's *Theory of Literary Production* (1966).

Macherey, in his analysis of the role of ideology in the production
of literature, argues that a literary text is produced within and
therefore aligned with the dominant ideology, and thus it conceals
the conditions of its own production. The word production is used
deliberately to suggest labour rather than inspiration. Following
Macherey, then the literary critic will tend to read past the 'obvious'
meaning of the text (such as the love story between Catherine and
Heathcliff) and look in the margins and gaps in the narrative for
evidence of the real conditions of its existence.

**CHECK
THE BOOK**

*Marxist Literary
Theory* edited by
Terry Eagleton and
Drew Milne (1996)
offers a superb
collection of Marxist
essays, giving a
good sense of the
historical formation
of a Marxist literary
tradition.

Taking this position, Musselwhite considers the 'normative' voices
of Lockwood and Nelly and also the pervasive imagery of books
and literature, all of which cooperate to render acceptable – as a love
story – what could otherwise have been a threatening tale of
rebellion and insubordination. The 'marginal' features of the
narration constitute what Musselwhite calls the 'unacceptable text'
of *Wuthering Heights*.

J. Hillis Miller has provided an influential deconstructive reading of
the novel. **Deconstruction** offers an alternative to traditional
scholarship which is both playful and openly adversarial. Unwilling
to privilege a certain kind of reading, deconstructive criticism argues
that there is no one right way to read a text, that literature does not
contain the kinds of unified and universal truths that traditional
criticism seeks. Instead deconstructive criticism considers the way
in which all **transcendental** truths, including those judgements we
might make about the aesthetic unity of the text, the inherent truth
of the narrative, undo themselves in internal contradictions and

incompatibilities. Miller's reading focuses upon the ways in which the novel resists rational explanation.

CONTEMPORARY APPROACHES

Evidently, and unsurprisingly, given its complex nature, *Wuthering Heights* has given rise to a plethora of readings.

MARXIST

Marxist criticisms of *Wuthering Heights* include Terry Eagleton's *Myths of Power: A Marxist Study of the Brontës* (1975); Arnold Kettle's *An Introduction to the English Novel* (1951); Margaret Lenta's essay 'Capitalism or Patriarchy and Immoral Love: A Study of *Wuthering Heights*' (1984); Raymond Williams's *The English Novel from Dickens to Lawrence* (1970) and David Wilson's essay 'Emily Brontë: First of the Moderns' (1947).

Terry Eagleton considers the novel in terms of its relationship to **ideology**. He uses Lucien Goldmann's definition of the term, which he admits is suspect, but, in terms of assessing *Wuthering Heights*, useful. Goldmann's definition is that ideology signifies a false, incomplete, distortive or partial consciousness, which he opposes to the term 'world-view' which designates a true, total and coherent understanding of social relations.

QUESTION

Does a notion of authentic love underpin any reading of this novel as a moral tragedy?

Wuthering Heights, argues Eagleton presents a 'world-view', in that it is unfragmented by the conflicts that it represents. Contradictions and contesting oppositions coexist in this novel in a profound but not unsatisfying tension.

The primary contradiction that Eagleton explores in relation to this assertion is the choice that Catherine must make between Edgar Linton and Heathcliff. He identifies that choice as the pivotal event of the novel and the precipitating factor in all the tragic events which follow. Catherine chooses Edgar Linton, which Eagleton identifies as an act of 'bad faith', because of his social superiority, and she is, he judges, rightly criticised by Heathcliff for this betrayal of their more authentic love. The social self, Eagleton argues, is demonstrated as false not because it is only apparent, Catherine's love for Edgar is not simulated, but because it exists in a contradictory and negative relationship to authentic selfhood, which is her love of Heathcliff.

Eagleton's essay also analyses Heathcliff's position in the novel in terms of his place in the family structure, local society and the economic system of rural Yorkshire at the turn of the century. Because Heathcliff is spirited out of nowhere into this family, he has no social or domestic status, and he is therefore both a threat to the established order and an opportunity for it to be reinvented. Heathcliff disturbs the establishment because he has no legitimate place in its system. Eagleton's analysis turns on the issue of liberty and oppression. The fact that there is no opportunity for freedom either within or outside the system is a consequence of bourgeois society.

Heathcliff learns to see culture as a mode of oppression, and he acquires it to use as a weapon. This association of culture with violence is further played out in the novel with the ferocity which is used to defend property, from the moment that Catherine is savaged by Skulker, the Linton's bulldog, to the complex wresting of property by Heathcliff in the second part of the novel.

QUESTION

What is the role of violence in this novel in which every character exhibits, or has the potential to exhibit, it?

In social terms the Heights can be read as embodying the world of the gentleman farmer: the petty-bourgeois yeoman, whereas the Grange epitomises the gentry. Eagleton argues that Heathcliff's social relation to both the Heights and the Grange is one of the most complex issues in the novel. Heathcliff fiercely highlights the contradictions between the two worlds in opposing the Grange and undermining the Heights. He embodies a passionate human protest against the marriage market values of both the Heights and the Grange, while violently caricaturing precisely those values in his calculatedly callous marriage to Isabella. In this Heathcliff can be seen to be a parody of capitalist activity, yet he is not simply this, for he is also a product of and participant in that system. The contradiction of the novel is that Heathcliff both embodies and antagonises the values which he wishes to contest.

The ending of the novel with its ostensible integration of the values of the two worlds might seem to qualify Eagleton's argument that the contradictions of the novel coexist in an exciting and productive tension. However, he argues that this conclusion depends upon how one reads Hareton Earnshaw. If Hareton is read as a surrogate and diluted Heathcliff, then the novel's ending does indeed suggest a reconciliation between the gentry and the capitalist. If however, Hareton is read as a literal survivor of yeoman stock, then what effectively happens is that he is entirely conquered by the **hegemony** of the Grange.

Eagleton concludes that the history of Catherine and Heathcliff is the history of a social and ideological opposition between the real and the ideal which demonstrates the terror and apathy of social conditions which deny passion, and equally displays the splendour and impotence of a love which has no social basis.

QUESTION

What are the relationships between clan, gender and labour in *Wuthering Heights*?

The opposition between love and marriage in this novel clearly identifies the conflicts between passion and possibility. Catherine identifies herself absolutely with Heathcliff: he is, more than any other character in this novel, her kin. Yet the existing social structures of class and capitalism refuse their relationship. It is not possible for Catherine as a desiring passionate subject to marry Heathcliff:

> did it never strike you that, if Heathcliff and I married, we should be beggars? Whereas if I marry Linton, I can aid Heathcliff to rise, and place him out of my brother's power.
>
> (Vol. 1, Ch. 9, p. 81)

Brontë is clear and unflinching here: for a woman to become socially powerful she is dependent upon finding a sexual mate whereby her submission brings her access to the dominant culture. However even this suggested promise of access to power, is qualified by Brontë when she has Nelly Dean respond: 'With your husband's money Miss Catherine? ... You'll find him not so pliable as you calculate upon...' (p. 81) and, indeed, the events of the novel bear this out. Brontë's decision to centralise the marriage of Catherine and Edgar thus emphasising the passion between Catherine and Heathcliff is

QUESTION

Adopting either a Marxist or a feminist perspective consider the role and significance of power in this novel.

revealing therefore both of the social structures which confine women within a patriarchal capitalist society and of an ideological interrogation of the dominant notions of love and marriage.

FEMINIST

Feminist criticism is a contested term. In her 1981 essay 'feminist criticism in the Wilderness', Elaine Showalter identified three common modes of feminist literary theory, and placed them as modes belonging to different national groups. She wrote:

> 'English feminist criticism, essentially Marxist, stresses oppression; French feminist criticism, essentially psychoanalytic, stresses repression; American feminist criticism, essentially textual, stresses expression. All, however, have become gynocentric. All are struggling to find a terminology that can rescue the feminine from its stereotypical associations with inferiority.'   (Showalter, 1986, p. 249)

Wuthering Heights has attracted feminist critics because: following early biographical criticism, it has been seen as drawing on the autobiographical experience of the author; because those experiences speak to our stereotyped ideas of Victorian femininity; and because it has an easily recovered historicist basis. For all these reasons it has been available for the **gynocritical** project of identifying a 'female tradition' of literature. Gynocentrism means woman-centredness.

Feminist readings of this novel include: Joseph Boone's *Tradition, Countertradition: Love and the Form of Fiction* (1987); Sandra Gilbert and Susan Gubar's *The Madwoman in the Attic: the Woman Writer and the Nineteenth-Century Literary Imagination* (1979); Margaret Homan's essay 'The Name of the Mother in *Wuthering Heights*' (1986); Carol Senf's essay 'Emily Brontë's version of Feminist History: *Wuthering Heights*' (1985); and Patricia Yaeger's essay 'Violence in the Sitting Room: *Wuthering Heights* and the Woman's Novel' (1988).

In *The Madwoman in the Attic*, Gilbert and Gubar interrogate *Wuthering Heights* in terms of what they term '**feminist** mythologies'. They see the project of the novel as rewriting and revising of the Miltonic myth of the Fall. They also identify the novel as a distinctively nineteenth-century response to the problems of origins, and as an exploration into the nature of heaven and hell.

In their reading of the novel in terms of writing against the male tradition, Gilbert and Gubar see *Wuthering Heights* as a 'Bible of Hell', a novel which validates the natural over the cultural, the anarchic over the world of organised repression. Wuthering Heights, the house of the title, is hellish by conventional standards, but for Catherine and Heathcliff it represents the kind of non-hierarchical social space in which they are permitted a degree of power which would be denied them elsewhere, since she is female and he is illegitimate, and they are both thereby excluded from power in the conventional world. Thrushcross Grange, across the moor, home of the Linton family, represents the standards of patriarchal culture which will be triumphant by the end of the story, but which the novel itself, through its sympathies for Catherine and Heathcliff, implicitly attacks.

> **CONTEXT**
>
> All feminist critical approaches to literature, whatever other traditions they borrow from, share a commitment to place women at the centre of the literary-critical discourses.

Their reading is spectacular, an omnibus of a reading, combining a traditional approach of close reading of the text with a wide-ranging citation of other critical sources and an assemblage of more miscellaneous detail. Its comprehensive accumulation of allusion makes it very powerful. For all its cogency and persuasiveness, however, this reading which forms part of their attempt to formulate a version of the female tradition is actually produced through parallel quotation and allusion. As Ruth Robbins (2000) acknowledges in her book *Literary Feminisms* 'The readings of particular texts are fascinating and important, but the conclusions about a female tradition drawn from larger contexts are open to question' (p. 92).

Nancy Armstrong's critique of their argument in *Desire and Domestic Fiction* argues that their approach is dangerously ahistorical and inasmuch as they deal with history, it is a history that takes place outside of women's sphere: 'For Gilbert and Gubar … history takes place not in and through those areas of culture over which women may have held sway, but in institutions dominated by men.' (1987, pp. 7–8).

Gilbert and Gubar's essay on *Wuthering Heights* sees the opposition of nature and culture in traditionally gendered terms, with culture as male, and nature as female. Indeed they assert that this novel is 'gender-obsessed'. Within the novel, a reading of the gendering of nature as female is supported by the manifestation of the storm as a female witch-child, the original Catherine, in Lockwood's second visionary dream. Heaven and hell are seen in similarly gendered terms. Catherine's choice of culture over nature, in marrying Edgar is overlaid by her assertion that she has 'no more business to marry Edgar Linton than I have to be in Heaven' (Vol. 1, Ch. 9, p. 80).

QUESTION

In what ways do the female characters of this novel mediate between nature and culture?

Their essay goes on to discuss the relationship between nature and culture in terms of Cathy and Heathcliff and their positions in the family structure. They read Heathcliff as the figurative manifestation of Catherine's desire for a whip. As Catherine's whip Heathcliff is an alternative self for her: 'a complementary addition to her being who fleshes out all her lacks' (p. 265). This is something Catherine herself recognises in her speech to Nelly Dean. Similarly Hindley's frustrated desire for a fiddle is symbolically fulfilled by his marriage to Frances.

This sustained gendered reading of the novel sees Thrushcross Grange as cultured and genteel, and the polar opposite of Wuthering Heights. That Catherine emerges from the Grange 'a lady' is seen as an inevitable consequence of subjection to masculine mythologies about heaven.

Focusing on the issue of naming in the novel, Gilbert and Gubar suggest that the writing of the name Catherine in its various manifestations, which Lockwood encounters inscribed into the windowsill, reveals the crucial lack of identity that is common to all women under patriarchy: 'What Catherine, or any girl must learn is that she does not know her own name, and therefore cannot know who she is or whom she is destined to be' (p. 276).

If Heathcliff is read as Catherine's complementary self, then, they argue Catherine's 'fall' into being a lady is accompanied by Heathcliff's diminution into a position of equally powerless femaleness. This reading of Heathcliff as female seems to go against the grain of conventional critical agreement that he epitomises heroic masculinity, especially when compared with the fair, slim, soft Edgar. But when these characters are read in terms of their social power, Heathcliff has no social position, and Edgar is always referred to as 'the master'. Edgar, who is most at home in the library, has all the power of masculine culture behind him. His mastery is contained in documents, books, rent-rolls, patriarchal domination. Edgar is the guardian of culture. Heathcliff is feminine in the sense that he is unpropertied, dispossessed, subject to the rule of the father, an outcast.

However, as Gilbert and Gubar point out, although Heathcliff can be read as Catherine's other self, he is not her identical double. This was a point first made by Leo Bersani in his book *A Future for Astyanax*. Not only is he male and she female, but he is a survivor, and usurper of power while she is a mournful, outcast, ghost. Nevertheless his fate at the end of the novel mirrors hers: he is unable to eat; he is feverish, and obsessed by the elements; and as is made clear in Gilbert and Gubar's argument, his death is partly as a result of his encounter with culture, in the form of Cathy, who embodies the intervention of patriarchy, as Edgar Linton's daughter. And in death, Heathcliff has arranged that his body shall merge with Catherine's until they are indistinguishable. Embedded in this argument about the reversals of structured meanings in the novel, they also try to establish relationships between *Wuthering Heights* and other kinds of texts, both male- and female-authored. Byron and Blake provide constant sources of reference, with Thrushcross Grange, for example being seen as an 'Urizenic' realm – a reference to Blake's unpleasantly righteous God figure Urizen; and with Heathcliff and Catherine's relationship being read in terms of Byron's verse drama *Manfred* (1817, a story of quasi-incestuous brother-sister love).

The logic of a female tradition, however, does not require this kind of absolute knowledge, since the female tradition is constructed both consciously in relation to known models and precursors and also unconsciously in relation to the shared experiences of oppression and the shared desire to protest, of the woman writer

CONTEXT

There is no evidence to the fact that Brontë had read Blake, though the Brontë sisters certainly read Byron compulsively.

Gilbert and Gubar's version of a female tradition looks both forwards and backwards. Gilbert and Gubar conclude that in writing *Wuthering Heights*, Emily Brontë struggled to subvert some of the founding myths of literature and religion, gender and marriage, patriarchy and power.

Other feminist critics also make the connections between the form of the novel and the historical position of women. They argue that the literary form is not politically innocent, but that 'discourses, sign-systems and signifying practices of all kinds … are closely related to the maintenance or transformation of our existing systems of power.'

Naomi Jacobs in 'Gender and Layered Narrative in *Wuthering Heights* and *The Tenant of Wildfell Hall*' (1986) gives a legal-social dimension to the question of the narrative frame, suggesting that the process of exposing the real constraints of women's lives represents at least a partial loosening of those constraints. The argument is that Brontë's challenging of the formal authoritative discourses of Victorian life, itself constitutes a radical intervention into those structures. She proceeds to document the prevalence of nineteenth-century wife-abuse and the reluctance of reviewers to acknowledge its existence – which she argues reveals the Brontë sisters as writing what was regarded as 'unwriteable' in contemporary terms. Jacobs then argues that the narrative structure of the novel represents an authorial strategy for dealing with the unacceptability of the subject matter.

CONTEXT

Jacob's article reminds us of the importance of the material, social aspect of *Wuthering Heights* as it relates to women.

STRUCTURALIST

'Structure' is a complex term, with many different uses, and can be used to refer to a number of features of a text. The aspect of *Wuthering Heights* which has generated the most persistent debate is what might be termed its 'narrative structure'; namely, the allocation of different parts of the story to different voices, rather than the more conventional narrative form in which one narrator tells his or her story.

Victorian reviewers criticised the novel for its confusing structure, since it confounded their belief that it was the novelist's duty to make his or her meaning plain. Evidently, the multitude of conflicting voices in this novel serves to disturb any such notions of clear meanings.

C. P. Sanger (1926) was among the first critics to argue that the structure of *Wuthering Heights* does in fact conform to a logical strictness and exactitude with regard to its dates and its probability of detail. He also argues that the most obvious thing about the structure of the story is the symmetry of the family pedigree: for Sanger, the whole intricate structure 'demonstrates the vividness of the author's imagination' (p. 20).

Knowing that a structure underlies apparent confusion, does not, however, make that confusion clearer. If as E.M. Forster asks in 1927 'she had a clear idea …Then why did she deliberately introduce muddle, chaos, tempest?' His own answer is revealing of the context in which he was writing: 'Because … she was a prophetess: because what is implied is more important to her than what is said.'

QUESTION

How does the structure of the family inform the structure of *Wuthering Heights*?

In 1930, William Empson published his text *Seven Types of Ambiguity*, arguing that ambiguity is at the very heart of poetic and therefore literary writing. The idea that ambiguity is a positive rather than a negative quality in writing has been immensely fruitful in all kinds of literary criticism, including the discussion of narrative structure.

Structuralist analyses of *Wuthering Heights* have included Lord David Cecil's 'storm and calm' reading and Dorothy Van Ghent's oppositions of inside and outside. Anthropological structuralism concerns itself particularly with kinship patterns, and Frank Kermode also begins his study of *Wuthering Heights* with an analysis of its proper names and family alliances, beginning from the names that Lockwood reads scratched on the window-sill.

PSYCHOANALYTIC

Psychoanalytic readings of *Wuthering Heights* have offered some very rich insights into this novel. Several Victorian critics, perhaps most famously Sidney Dobell (1850), saw the exciting possibilities of considering *Wuthering Heights* as a study in abnormal psychology. Freudian psychoanalytic theory, however, offers critics a more precise vocabulary and a more robust explanation for obsessive and divided mentalities, and therefore has proved fruitful for subsequent readers.

Thomas Moser was the first to adopt a clearly and uncompromisingly Freudian analysis of *Wuthering Heights* in his essay, 'What is the Matter with Emily Jane?' published in 1962. Moser's argument is that in the figures of Catherine and Heathcliff, Brontë dramatised what Freud was to subsequently call the id, that unknown, repressed and childish part of everyone: 'The primary traits which Freud ascribed to the id apply perfectly to Heathcliff: the source of psychic energy; the seat of the instincts (particularly sex and death); the essence of dreams; the archaic foundation of personality – selfish, asocial, impulsive' (p. 4).

Feminist critics have frequently made use of psychoanalytical theory. In *Women, the Longest Revolution* (1966) Juliet Mitchell points out that Brontë's subjects, like Freud's, were 'infancy, adolescence, early childhood and death' (p. 128).

However, most contemporary feminist theorists reject Freud's identification of the experience of women as essentially tragic, following her discovery of her 'lack' of a penis.

As Freudian theory became contested and divided between increasingly incompatible disciples, so there are studies of *Wuthering Heights* from a variety of post-Freudian positions. Many feminist theorists have turned to the theories of Jacques Lacan to inform their psychoanalytic readings. For example, Anne Williams, in her essay, 'The Child is *Mother* of the Man' published in 1991, demonstrates how Freud's theory of the Oedipal crisis can be adapted, by way of Lacan, to suit feminist readers. She argues that the appeal of the central love story between Catherine and Heathcliff can be understood by recognising that this love represents the stage of development psychoanalysts call the pre-Oedipal.

CHECK THE BOOK

There are a number of very good Critical Readers which offer a selection of critical essays and suggest the links between them. Douglas Tallack (ed): *Critical Theory: A Reader*, 1995 has a useful section on psychoanalytical theory.

The pre-Oedipal period is a period of time of absolute identification between the self and someone else (usually the mother). It is a period of time which precedes separation from the mother, acquisition of language and self-consciousness. Communication at this stage is a communion which has no need of words. It is clear that such a theoretical position has much to offer in the reading of the relationship between the 'motherless orphans' Catherine and Heathcliff.

The later Oedipal Crisis requires that the child adopt a culture and language, and this demands separation from, and repression of, the mother (and all culture associated with her).

Juliet Mitchell (1984) takes up this idea and argues:

> the choices for the woman within the novel, ... are either to survive by making the hysteric's ambiguous choice into a femininity which doesn't work (marrying Edgar) or to go for ... unity, ... suffering death, walking the moors as a ghost with Heathcliff. (p. 293)

Because of its nature the unconscious is normally inaccessible to the conscious mind. Therefore we must pay attention to the secret ways in which it might reveal itself. One of these ways is through the analysis of dreams, and one of Freud's earliest published works was *The Interpretation of Dreams* (1900). With its emphasis upon dreams that disrupt the smooth flowing of the narrative, and which are hard to assimilate into the main body of the text, *Wuthering Heights* has proved rich territory for dream interpretation.

As Patsy Stoneman (1993) points out in her Reader's Guide, one of the first critics to attend to dreams in *Wuthering Heights* was Edith Maud Fenton in 1920. Fenton was concerned to establish the dreams as a means of distinguishing *Wuthering Heights* from the conventional Gothic novel. Whereas in the Gothic novel dreams are 'definitely useful' – inasmuch as they indicate solutions to problems – those in *Wuthering Heights*, Fenton argues, contain the 'revelation of personality, the vision of unsatisfied longings, the pathos of the unattainable in life.' (pp. 107, 109–10)

? QUESTION

Consider Catherine's famous declaration of love to Nelly: 'Nelly, I <u>am</u> Heathcliff' (p. 82) from the perspective of psychoanalytic theory.

As Stoneman notes however, most studies of the dreams in this novel do try to make them 'useful' in interpreting the text.

William A. Madden's article '*Wuthering Heights*: The Binding of Passion', published in 1972, argues, through an analysis of the dreams and visions as indicative of Brontë's values and moral stance, that Joseph is the 'villain' of *Wuthering Heights*. Following Edgar F. Shannon who argued that Branderham's text is Matthew 18:21–2, Madden argues that each of the subjects in the dream – Joseph, Lockwood and Branderham, misconstrue the symbolic meaning of Jesus's words when he says that we should pardon a brother's sin seventy times seven times, interpreting them literally rather than as a command to practice 'unlimited forgiveness':

> Although the precise nature of the unforgivable sin has been debated, Emily Brontë makes it clear that for her the unforgivable sin consists in judging the human offences of others as unforgivable.
>
> (p. 131)

QUESTION

With reference to Lockwood's dream, to what extent do any of the characters in *Wuthering Heights* practice forgiveness?

Madden (1972) argues that the quality of rigid 'unforgivingness' is particularly associated with Joseph and therefore orthodox religion. He argues that Joseph deliberately turns Mr Earnshaw against each of his children (p. 135). Following this, Madden sees the second part of the story, with the younger Catherine as both strong and necessary to the development of the themes. Lockwood's dream then becomes a key to understanding the rest of the novel, and as such is crucial to its structure.

Freud's hypothesis was that all dreams represent a wish-fulfilment. He argued that the purpose of dreaming was to gratify this need for wish-fulfilment. He qualified this in the cases where there was evidence that children or adults had been traumatised. In these cases, dreams compulsively return to the source of the neurosis in an attempt to 'bind' the excess of emotion. Dreaming then becomes a way of 'containing' trauma. This effort is usually unsuccessful and the sufferers instead evade the problem by returning to a state prior to the trauma. Madden posits that in *Wuthering Heights* the central defining trauma for Catherine and Heathcliff is their exclusion from the Earnshaw family an exclusion which is grimly presided over by

Joseph. He argues that following this exclusion their attachment for each other and their obsessive 'love' is 'rooted in their radical alienation' and is thus incapable of any positive development (p. 150). In an extensive and generous analysis of Cathy's moral courage in the second volume, as she confronts Heathcliff's tyrannical oppression and forges an alliance with Hareton, Madden argues that she and Hareton succeed in 'binding' their emotion so that it is 'channelled into human wholeness and health through the transforming power of a love that both understands and forgives.' (p. 154).

Many contemporary psychoanalytical studies of *Wuthering Heights* derive not from Freud but from the theories of Jacques Lacan, whose ideas have been of particular interest to literary critics because of their focus on language. Philip K. Wion presents the absence of mothers as a pathological feature of *Wuthering Heights*, which can be attributed to the fact that Emily Brontë's mother died when she was three. Lacan theorises such mother-loss as absolutely constitutive of the human condition.

The effect of Jacques Lacan's work upon literary theory has been to establish a powerful intellectual tradition that focuses its attention almost exclusively upon the centrality of language.

For Lacan, infants acquire language at precisely the point where they realise that the mother's body is not exclusively theirs or identical with theirs. Language thus originates in loss, a sign of absence and immediately recognises the Other. Wion's argument that the Catherine-Heathcliff relationship attempts to replicate the pre-linguistic relationship between mother and child is Lacanian in its mode and its emphasis upon language.

One of the most significant and influential discussions of *Wuthering Heights* in this context is in Leo Bersani's book *A Future for Astyanax* (1976). Accepting the Freudian/Lacanian argument that individual identity is always constructed within the family, Bersani reads the novel in terms of how difficult it is 'to locate and define human identity' (p. 197).

CHECK THE BOOK

For a further example of a specifically Lacanian approach to *Wuthering Heights* see Margaret Homan's essay: In 'Dreaming of Children: Literalization in *Jane Eyre* and *Wuthering Heights*' (1983).

Bersani argues that the 'frenzy of *Wuthering Heights* is the result of Heathcliff's sudden appearance in the middle of a family whose members know who they are, where they came from, what they belong to' (p. 205). Arguing against the grain of conventional readings, Bersani insists that Catherine is not 'like' Heathcliff – arguing that where she is sociable, hectic, and mobile; he is closed and silent.

Bersani draws on two aspects of Lacanian theory – the mirror phase and the 'fort-da' game to examine Heathcliff's function in the novel.

The 'mirror phase' marks the first stage of separation between the mother and child. Until the child sees its reflection in a mirror it has no concept of its own separateness. Up until this point the child perceives itself to be contiguous with the mother, and with the world. For Lacan the mirror phase is critical because it precedes language and mature identity, but nevertheless resides in our (pre)consciousness as a sort of proto-memory of a blissful 'Imaginary' identity with an 'other' who both is and is not the self. It is the stage of what Lacan calls the 'Ideal-I'.

> **CONTEXT**
>
> Lacan's identification of the 'Ideal-I' adopts Freud's term the 'Ideal-Ich'.

Following this, the rest of our adult life is a search for metaphorical 'mirrors' in order to confirm our sense of who we are.

The 'fort-da' game was extrapolated from Freud's experience of watching his infant grandson playing a game by lowering a cotton reel on a piece of string. As the child watched the toy appear and disappear, he cried out 'fort' (gone) and 'da' (here). The satisfaction gained from the language here demonstrates for Lacan that language appears to fill the gap left by the absent object. Combining these two theories Bersani argues that the mirror is also:

> a spatial representation of an intuition that our being can never be adequately enclosed within any present formulation ... of our being ...Thus although it is ourselves we see in the mirror, the experience can paradoxically be considered as a model for our imagination of being very different from ourselves. *Wuthering Heights* represents the danger of being haunted by alien versions of the self.
> (p. 208)

PART FIVE

BACKGROUND

EMILY BRONTË

Emily Brontë was born in 1818 in Yorkshire. Her father, Patrick Brontë, was curate of Haworth Parsonage. In 1821 Emily's mother died and, following the deaths of two elder sisters in 1825 the surviving children, Charlotte, Emily, Anne and Branwell were brought up by their aunt in the parsonage. They lived relatively remotely from their community, and Charlotte explains in the biographical notice which prefaces most editions of the text, that they took their chief enjoyment from literary compositions which they invented for each other most famously the sagas of the mythical island of Gondal which inspired their later poetry. Patrick Brontë fostered in his children a spirit of intellectual enquiry and a love of literature, they had access to his library and to the nearby library in Keighley. Emily briefly attended Cowan Bridge School and went to Row Head in 1835.

Following Charlotte's discovery of her poetry notebooks Emily agreed to publish a book of poems jointly with her sisters, which they published in 1846 under the **pseudonyms** Currer, Ellis and Acton Bell.

Wuthering Heights is Emily's only novel and was published under the pseudonym Ellis Bell in 1847, a year before her death from tuberculosis.

HER OTHER WORKS

Emily Brontë published only one other work during her lifetime, which was a joint publication of poetry with her sisters. Although this book did not achieve critical acclaim, Charlotte remained convinced of the quality of Emily's verse and in the 1850 edition of *Wuthering Heights*, included some of Emily's verse as an appendix. This brought it to the attention of many readers, including the American poet Emily Dickinson (1830–86), who particularly admired the poem 'No Coward Soul', which was read at

> **CONTEXT**
>
> The fact that formal education in *Wuthering Heights* is almost invariably represented as a fearful, even traumatic experience has been attributed to Emily Brontë's own experience at the Clergy Daughters' School.

Dickinson's funeral. This inclusion of the poetry with the novel focused readers' attention on the poetic qualities of her prose writing.

HISTORICAL BACKGROUND

Although critics are divided in their opinions as to the usefulness of an historical context for an understanding of *Wuthering Heights*, some, like Terry Eagleton, Arnold Kettle and Nancy Armstrong have focused acute critical attention upon the economic and social conditions which inform the novel, seeing the novel as both a product of and participant in the social context.

Certainly, Victorian readers would have been familiar with the story of Heathcliff as a foundling from the port of Liverpool: orphans and child beggars were a common enough social problem. Heathcliff's background, tantalisingly obscure as it might seem within the novel, can be read against the social upheavals of the mid nineteenth century, which saw unemployment as a result of industrialisation; the Irish potato famine which brought thousands of refugees to Liverpool; the decay of a rural lifestyle in the face of increased urbanisation and new technology. The **romantic** and nostalgic references to nature and to the moors as a place of childhood might also be read in this context. However, as Eva Figes points out in *Sex and Subterfuge, Women Writers in 1850* (Pandora, 1982) Victorian women writers had been largely prevented from writing social or political criticism in their novels owing to their vulnerable position as women writers. The rural setting of *Wuthering Heights* can be seen as indicative of the position of women as isolated from culture and modern industry. The emphasis upon the struggle between nature and culture, north and south, folklore and science, can be recognised as being particularly disturbing to its contemporary readership.

CHECK THE BOOK

Elizabeth Gaskell's biography of Charlotte Brontë (1857) makes it very clear that the Brontë sisters struggled with the conflict between being a woman and being a writer.

Emphasis upon a literary context for the novel has been twofold. First, critics have pointed out the poetic qualities of the novel and have cited the influence of Byron. Indeed it has become a critical commonplace to read Heathcliff as a **Byronic hero**. The Byronic influences have been particularly discussed by Winifred Gérin in her biography of Brontë. A second source of influence has been considered to be the **gothic** romance, and critics have seen the influence of ghosts and visions in this context. The gothic romance was a popular form of writing in the late eighteenth and nineteenth centuries. It generally dealt with the supernatural and the fantastic. Heathcliff's desire for Catherine which extends beyond the grave can be seen in this context. Gilbert and Gubar (1979) famously suggest the possibility of *Wuthering Heights* as a 'deliberate copy' of Mary Shelley's *Frankenstein*. Nancy Armstrong, though, suggests that such phenomena might also be read in terms of the competing discourses of folklore and literature.

QUESTION

With reference to Psychoanalytic or Feminist theory, formulate your response to Isabella's question: 'Is Mr Heathcliff a man? If so, is he mad? And if not, is he a devil?' (Vol. I, Ch. 13, p. 134).

History	Author's life	Literature
		1811 Jane Austen, *Sense and Sensibility*
		1817 Lord Byron, *Manfred*. Sir Walter Scott, *Rob Roy*
	1818 Born in Yorkshire the fifth of six children	**1818** Mary Shelley, *Frankenstein*. Lord Byron, *Childe Harold* (Canto IV)
	1821 Her mother dies and she is sent to Cowan Bridge School as a boarder	**1819–24** Lord Byron, *Don Juan*
1825 First passenger railway opens	**1825** Emily's two elder sisters die of consumption at Cowan Bridge School and Emily and her sister Charlotte return to Haworth where they are brought up by their aunt	
1834 Parish workhouses introduced. Abolition of slavery in territories governed by Britain		**1830** William Cobbett, *Rural Rides*
	1835 Attends Roe Head School to study to become a teacher but is physically homesick and returns to Haworth	
1837 The Victorian era begins. Victoria becomes Queen	**1837** Spends six months as a governess at a girls' boarding school at Law Hill near Halifax, before returning home through ill health	
1838–42 Chartism is at its peak of popularity		**1838** Elizabeth Barrett Browning, *The Seraphim and Other Poems*
1842 Employment in mines of women and children under ten is outlawed. Chartist uprising	**1842** Goes to Brussels with Charlotte but aunt dies and they return home	
	1846 Emily and her sisters publish a book of poems under the pseudonyms Currer, Ellis and Acton Bell	
	1847 *Wuthering Heights*	
	1848 Brother Bramwell dies; Emily dies from tuberculosis	**1848** Robert Browning, *Dramatic Lyrics*
		1857 Elizabeth Gaskell *The Life of Charlotte Brontë*

FURTHER READING

THE TEXT

Heather Glen, ed., *Wuthering Heights*, Routledge, 1988

Hilda Marsden and Ian Jack, eds, *Wuthering Heights*, Clarendon Press, 1976

Linda H. Peterson, ed., *Wuthering Heights: Case Studies in Contemporary Criticism*, Bedford Books of St. Martin's Press, 1992

William M. Sale Jr and Richard J. Dunn, eds, *Wuthering Heights*: A Norton Critical Edition, 3rd edition, W.W. Norton, 1990

Emily Brontë, *The Complete Poems*, ed. Derek Roper with Edward Chitham, Clarendon Press, 1995

BIOGRAPHY

Juliet Barker, *The Brontës*, Weidenfield & Nicholson, 1994

Edward Chitham, *A Life of Emily Brontë*, Basil Blackwell, 1987

Elizabeth Gaskell, *The Life of Charlotte Brontë*, Smith, Elder & Co., London, 1857, reprinted by Penguin Books, 1975

Winifred Gérin, *Emily Brontë*, Clarendon Press, 1971

Katherine Frank, *Emily Brontë: A Chainless Soul*, H. Hamilton, 1990, paperback, Penguin Books, Harmondsworth, 1992

A. Mary F. Robinson, *Emily Brontë*, W.H. Allen, 1883

CRITICAL WORKS

Miriam Allott, ed., *Emily Brontë: Wuthering Heights: A Selection of Critical Essays*, Macmillan, 1970

Miriam Allott, ed., *The Brontës: The Critical Heritage*, Routledge & Kegan Paul, 1974

Nancy Armstrong, *Desire and Domestic Fiction: A Political History of the Novel*, Oxford University Press, 1987

Nancy Armstrong 'Imperialist Nostalgia and *Wuthering Heights*' in Linda H. Peterson, ed., *Wuthering Heights: Case Studies in Contemporary Criticism*, 1992

Trevor J. Barnes and James S. Duncan, eds, *Writing Worlds: Discourse, Text and Metaphor*, Routledge & Kegan Paul, 1992

Roland Barthes, 'An Introduction to the Structural Analysis of Narrative' trans. Lionel Dusit *New Literary History* 6 (Winter 1975)

Roland Barthes, *Image – Music –Text*, trans. S. Heath, Fontana, London, 1977

Peter Bayne, 'Ellis, Acton and Currer Bell' *Essays in Biography and Criticism*, first series, 1857

Catherine Belsey, *Critical Practice*, Routledge, 1980

Leo Bersani, *A Future for Astyanax: Character and Desire in Literature*, Little, 1976

Harold Bloom, ed., *Emily Brontë's Wuthering Heights*, Chelsea, 1987

Harold Bloom, ed., *Modern Critical Views: The Brontës*, New York, Chelsea House, 1987

Joseph Allen Boone, *Tradition, Countertradition: Love and the Form of Fiction*, University of Chicago Press, 1987

Elisabeth Bronfen, *Over Her Dead Body: Death, Femininity and the Aesthetic*, Manchester University Press, 1992

Mary Burgan, 'Some Fit Parentage: Identity and the Cycle of Generations in *Wuthering Heights*', *Philological Quarterly* 61:4 (Fall 1982) pp. 395–413

Lord David Cecil, *Early Victorian Novelists: Essays in Revaluation*, revised edition, University of Chicago Press, 1958. Originally published 1935

Helene Cixous, 'The Laugh of the Medusa' *New French Feminisms* in Elaine Marks and Isabelle de Courtivron, eds, University of Massachusetts Press, 1980

Jay Clayton, *Romantic Vision and The Novel*, Cambridge University Press, 1987

Stevie Davies, *Emily Brontë: The Artist as a Free Woman*, Carcanet Press, 1983

Jacques Derrida, *Specters of Marx*, trans. Peggy Kamuf, Routledge, 1994

Sydney Dobell, 'Currer Bell and *Wuthering Heights*', Palladium, (September 1850)

Terry Eagleton, *Myths of Power: A Marxist Study of the Brontës*, Harper & Row, 1975, 2nd edition, Macmillan, 1992

Terry Eagleton, *Literary Theory An Introduction*, Oxford University Press, 1983

Terry Eagleton and Drew Milne, eds, *Marxist Literary Theory*, Blackwell, 1996

William Empson, *Seven Types of Ambiguity*, Chatto & Windus, 1930

John P. Farrell, 'Reading the Text of Community in *Wuthering Heights*', *ELH* 56:1 (Spring 1989)

Edith Maud Fenton, 'The Spirit of Emily Brontë's *Wuthering Heights* as Distinguished from That of Gothic Romances', Washington University Studies, Humanities Series 8 (1920) pp. 103-22

Eva Figes, *Sex and Subterfuge, Women Writers in 1850*, Pandora, 1982

Juliann E. Fleenor, ed., *The Female Gothic*, Eden Press, 1983

E.M. Forster, *Aspects of the Novel*, Edward Arnold, 1927

Sigmund Freud, *The Interpretation of Dreams*, Penguin, first Penguin edition 1953

Sandra Gilbert and Susan Gubar, *The Madwoman in the Attic: The Woman Writer and the Nineteenth-Century Literary Imagination*, Yale University Press, 1979

Elliot Gose, *Imagination Indulg'd*, Queen's University Press, 1972

Ian Gregor, ed., *The Brontës: A Collection of Critical Essays*, Prentice-Hall, 1970

James Hafley, 'The Villain in *Wuthering Heights*', *Nineteenth-Century Fiction* 13 (December 1958)

Barbara Hardy, *Forms of Feeling in Victorian Fiction*, Peter Owen, 1985

Margaret Homans 'Repression and Sublimation of Nature in *Wuthering Heights*', *PMLA* 93 (January 1978)

Margaret Homans, *Women Writers and Poetic Identity: Dorothy Wordsworth, Emily Brontë and Emily Dickinson*, Princeton University Press, 1980

Margaret Homans, 'Dreaming of Children: Literalization in *Jane Eyre* and *Wuthering Heights*'. In Juliann E. Fleenor, ed., *The Female Gothic*, Eden Press, 1983

Margaret Homans, '*The Name of the Mother in Wuthering Heights*'. Bearing the Word: *Language and Female Experience in Nineteenth-Century Women's Writing*, University of Chicago Press, 1986

Carol Jacobs: '*Wuthering Heights*: At the Threshold of Interpretation' *boundary* 2, 7 (Spring 1979)

Naomi Jacobs, 'Gender and Layered Narrative in *Wuthering Heights* and *The Tenant of Wildfell Hall*', *Journal of Narrative Technique* 16:3 (Fall 1986)

Frederic Jameson, *The Political Unconscious*, Cornell University Press, 1981

E. Jolly, ed., *The Life and Letters of Sydney Dobell*, volume 1, Smith, 1878

Arnold Kettle, *An Introduction to the English Novel*, volume 1, Hutchinson, 1951; revised edition, Heinemann Educational and Open University Press, 1981

Frank Kermode, *The Classic*, Faber & Faber, 1975

Robert Kiely, *The Romantic Novel in England*, Harvard University Press, 1972

Julia Kristeva, *Revolution in Poetic Language* trans. Margaret Waller, Columbia University Press, 1984. Originally published 1974

F.R Leavis, *The Great Tradition: George Eliot, Henry James, Joseph Conrad*, Penguin, 1962

F.R. Leavis and Q.D. Leavis, *Lectures in America*, Pantheon Books, 1969

Q.D. Leavis, *Fiction and the Reading Public*, Chatto & Windus, 1932

Q.D. Leavis, 'A Fresh Approach to *Wuthering Heights*' in G. Singh, ed., *Collected Essays* (Vol. 1), Cambridge University Press, 1983–9. Essay originally published 1969

Margaret Lenta, 'Capitalism or Patriarchy and Immoral Love: A Study of *Wuthering Heights*', *Theoria: A Journal of Studies in the Arts, Humanities and Social Sciences* 62 (1984) pp. 63–76

Pierre Macherey, *A Theory of Literary Production*, Routledge and Kegan Paul, 1966

William A. Madden, '*Wuthering Heights*, The Binding of Passion', *Nineteenth Century Fiction* 27 (1972) pp. 127–54

John K. Matthison, 'Nelly Dean and the Power of *Wuthering Heights*' *Nineteenth-Century Fiction* 11 (1956)

Peter Miles, *The Critics Debate: Wuthering Heights*, London, Macmillan, 1990

J. Hillis Miller, *Fiction and Repetition*, Harvard University Press and Basil Blackwell, 1982

Sara Mills, Lynne Pearce, Susan Spaull, Elaine Millard, eds *Feminist Readings, Feminists Reading*, Harvester Wheatsheaf, 1989

Juliet Mitchell, *Women, The Longest Revolution: Essays on Feminism, Literature and Psychoanalysis*, Virago, 1984

Thomas Moser, 'What is the Matter with Emily Jane? Conflicting Impulses in *Wuthering Heights*', *Nineteenth-Century Fiction* 17 (June 1962)

David Musselwhite, '*Wuthering Heights*: The Unacceptable Text' in Francis Barker et al. *Literature, Society and the Sociology of Literature*, University of Essex Press, 1977. Essay originally published 1976

Bernard Paris, 'Hush, Hush! He's a Human Being: A Psychological Approach to Heathcliff', *Women and Literature* 2 (1982)

Ruth Robbins, *Literary Feminisms*, Macmillan, 2000

Rick Rylance, ed., *Debating Texts*, OUP, 1987

C.P. Sanger, *The Structure of 'Wuthering Heights'*, Hogarth Press, 1926

Ferdinand de Saussure, *Course in General Linguistics*, London, 1983

Barbara Schapiro, 'The Rebirth of Catherine Earnshaw: Splitting and Regeneration of the Self in *Wuthering Heights*', *Nineteenth Century Studies* 3 (1989) pp. 37-51

Mark Schorer, 'Fiction and the Matrix of Analogy' *The Kenyon Review* 11:4 (Autumn 1949)

Carol A. Senf, 'Emily Brontë's version of Feminist History: *Wuthering Heights*', Essays in Literature 12 (1985) pp. 201–14

Edgar F. Shannon Jr, 'Lockwood's Dreams and the Exegesis of *Wuthering Heights*', *Nineteenth Century Fiction* 14 (September 1959) pp. 95–110

Elaine Showalter, *A Literature of Their Own: British Women Novelists from Brontë to Lessing*, Princeton University Press, 1977; revised edition, Virago, 1984

Elaine Showalter, *Sexual Anarchy: Gender and Culture at the Fin de Siecle*, Bloomsbury, 1991

Susan Sontag, *Illness as Metaphor. Aids and its Metaphors*, Penguin, 1991

Patsy Stoneman, ed., *Wuthering Heights, Contemporary Critical Essays*, Macmillan, 1993

Julia Swindells, *Victorian Writing and Working Women*, University of Minnesota Press, 1985

Wade Thomson, 'Infanticide and Sadism in *Wuthering Heights*', *PMLA* 78:1 (March 1963)

Dorothy Van Ghent, 'The Window Figure and the Two Children Figure in *Wuthering Heights*', *Nineteenth-Century Fiction* 7 (December 1952)

Dorothy Van Ghent, *The English Novel: Form and Function*, Harper Torchbooks, 1961

Mary Visick, *The Genesis of Wuthering Heights*, Hong Kong University Press/Oxford University Press, 1958; 3rd edition, Ian Hodgkins, 1980

Marina Warner, *From the Beast to the Blonde*, Chatto & Windus, 1994

Anne Williams, 'The Child is Mother to the Man': The Female Aesthetic of *Wuthering Heights*', *Cahiers Victoriens et Edouardiens* 34 (October 1991)

FURTHER READING

Raymond Williams, *The English Novel from Dickens to Lawrence*, Chatto & Windus, 1970

Raymond Williams, *The Country and The City*, Chatton & Windus, 1973

David Wilson, '*Emily Brontë*: First of the Moderns,' *Modern Quarterly Miscellany* 1 (1947) pp. 94–115

Philip K. Wion, 'The Absent Mother in Emily Brontë's *Wuthering Heights*', *American Imago* 42 (1985)

Carl Woodring, 'The Narrators of *Wuthering Heights*', *Nineteenth-Century Fiction* 11 (1957)

Patricia Yaeger, 'Violence in the Sitting Room: *Wuthering Heights* and the Woman's Novel', *Genre* 21 (1988) pp. 203–29 biographical criticism a critical approach which focuses upon the relationship between fiction and reality by drawing upon the author's life-story

Byronic hero characteristically both glamorous and dangerous, haunted by the guilt of mysterious crimes

deconstruction a post-structuralist approach to literature initiated by the theoretical ideas of Jacques Derrida. Deconstruction posits the radical undecidability of all texts

discourse discourse theory is associated with the writings of Michel Foucault. Discourse generally refers to the language in which a specific area of knowledge is discussed, e.g. the discourse of law or medicine

feminist criticism there are many different forms of feminist criticism: some critics suggest ways of reading which draw attention to the patriarchal assumptions underpinning cultural production; others focus on the rediscovery of works by women writers; still others concentrate on the psychological and linguistic opportunities for women in a male-dominated culture

formalism also known as new criticism, formalists concentrate on the formal structure of the text, particularly such elements as imagery, symbolism, repetition

gothic a genre of writing which has a number of typical elements such ghosts, horror, sublime landscapes

gynocriticism a term which refers to the practice of turning away from the analysis of male-authored texts to an analysis of female-authored texts and heir specific differences from one another

hegemony associated with the political writings of Antonio Gramsci, hegemony refers to the web of ideologies that shape people's view of the world

hermeneutics the art or science of interpretation

ideology a set of beliefs about the world which seems both natural and inevitable.

marxist criticism a way of reading texts that focuses upon their material and historical conditions

metaphysical visionary writing, generally associated with the seventeenth century. Incorporeal, abstract

new criticism see formalism

new historicism a form of criticism heavily influenced by Marxist criticism and the work of Michel Foucault. Foucault's notion of 'power' and 'discourse' were particularly formative of New Historicist thinking.

palimpsest a text that is overwritten with other narratives and messages

parable a story which explains something which cannot easily be rendered otherwise

post-structuralism both a continuation and a critique of structuralism. Post-structuralist criticism expands the possibilities of language: the binary oppositions central to a structuralist position proliferate into innumerable alternatives. In post-structuralist readings meaning is never stable and uncontrovertible, but always provisional and contradictory

pseudonym an adopted name under which to write

psychoanalytic criticism a way of considering texts in terms of the psychoanalytic theories of Sigmund Freud. Emphasis upon dream analysis. Later psychoanalytic theory takes account of the work of Jacques Lacan, especially his theories of language

romantic a literary form characterised by a conscious preoccupation with the subjective and imaginative aspects of life

semiotics the study of signs and sign systems. Associated particularly with the work of Ferdinand de Saussure

structuralism structuralist criticism derives from the linguistic theory of Saussure. It focuses on the internal structures of language which permit a text to 'mean' something. A structuralist analysis posits language rather than an individual author as the creator of meaning – no word has intrinsic meaning, in and of itself – it only means something in relation to other words. This insight is discussed chiefly in terms of binary oppositions. We understand what 'hot' means only in relation to the term 'cold'. According to structuralists writing has no origin – every individual utterance is already preceded by language

transcendent often synonymous with metaphysical – that which is beyond the limits of human cognition; exceeding or surpassing the ordinary

Claire Jones attended the Universities of Sussex and Oxford. She has taught in Cape Town and Oxford, and was a lecturer in English literary studies at the University of Luton, where she specialised in literary theory and contemporary literature.

General editor

Martin Gray, former Head of the Department of English Studies at the University of Stirling, and of Literary Studies at the University of Luton.

Maya Angelou
I Know Why the Caged Bird Sings

Jane Austen
Pride and Prejudice

Alan Ayckbourn
Absent Friends

Elizabeth Barrett Browning
Selected Poems

Robert Bolt
A Man for All Seasons

Harold Brighouse
Hobson's Choice

Charlotte Brontë
Jane Eyre

Emily Brontë
Wuthering Heights

Shelagh Delaney
A Taste of Honey

Charles Dickens
David Copperfield
Great Expectations
Hard Times
Oliver Twist

Roddy Doyle
Paddy Clarke Ha Ha Ha

George Eliot
Silas Marner
The Mill on the Floss

Anne Frank
The Diary of a Young Girl

William Golding
Lord of the Flies

Oliver Goldsmith
She Stoops to Conquer

Willis Hall
The Long and the Short and the Tall

Thomas Hardy
Far from the Madding Crowd
The Mayor of Casterbridge
Tess of the d'Urbervilles
The Withered Arm and other Wessex Tales

L.p. Hartley
The Go-Between

Seamus Heaney
Selected Poems

Susan Hill
I'm the King of the Castle

Barry Hines
A Kestrel for a Knave

Louise Lawrence
Children of the Dust

Harper Lee
To Kill a Mockingbird

Laurie Lee
Cider with Rosie

Arthur Miller
The Crucible
A View from the Bridge

Robert O'Brien
Z for Zachariah

Frank O'Connor
My Oedipus Complex and Other Stories

George Orwell
Animal Farm

J.B. Priestley
An Inspector Calls
When We Are Married

Willy Russell
Educating Rita
Our Day Out

J.D. Salinger
The Catcher in the Rye

William Shakespeare
Henry IV Part I
Henry V
Julius Caesar
Macbeth
The Merchant of Venice
A Midsummer Night's Dream
Much Ado About Nothing

Romeo and Juliet
The Tempest
Twelfth Night

George Bernard Shaw
Pygmalion

Mary Shelley
Frankenstein

R.C. Sherriff
Journey's End

Rukshana Smith
Salt on the snow

John Steinbeck
Of Mice and Men

Robert Louis Stevenson
Dr Jekyll and Mr Hyde

Jonathan Swift
Gulliver's Travels

Robert Swindells
Daz 4 Zoe

Mildred D. Taylor
Roll of Thunder, Hear My Cry

Mark Twain
Huckleberry Finn

James Watson
Talking in Whispers

Edith Wharton
Ethan Frome

William Wordsworth
Selected Poems

A Choice of Poets

Mystery Stories of the Nineteenth Century including The Signalman

Nineteenth Century Short Stories

Poetry of the First World War

Six Women Poets

For the AQA Anthology:

Duffy and Armitage & Pre-1914 Poetry

Heaney and Clarke & Pre-1914 Poetry

Poems from Different Cultures

Margaret Atwood
Cat's Eye
The Handmaid's Tale

Jane Austen
Emma
Mansfield Park
Persuasion
Pride and Prejudice
Sense and Sensibility

Alan Bennett
Talking Heads

William Blake
Songs of Innocence and of Experience

Charlotte Brontë
Jane Eyre
Villette

Emily Brontë
Wuthering Heights

Angela Carter
Nights at the Circus

Geoffrey Chaucer
The Franklin's Prologue and Tale
The Merchant's Prologue and Tale
The Miller's Prologue and Tale
The Prologue to the Canterbury Tales
The Wife of Bath's Prologue and Tale

Samuel Coleridge
Selected Poems

Joseph Conrad
Heart of Darkness

Daniel Defoe
Moll Flanders

Charles Dickens
Bleak House
Great Expectations
Hard Times

Emily Dickinson
Selected Poems

John Donne
Selected Poems

Carol Ann Duffy
Selected Poems

George Eliot
Middlemarch
The Mill on the Floss

T.S. Eliot
Selected Poems
The Waste Land

F. Scott Fitzgerald
The Great Gatsby

E.M. Forster
A Passage to India

Brian Friel
Translations

Thomas Hardy
Jude the Obscure
The Mayor of Casterbridge
The Return of the Native
Selected Poems
Tess of the d'Urbervilles

Seamus Heaney
Selected Poems from 'Opened Ground'

Nathaniel Hawthorne
The Scarlet Letter

Homer
The Iliad
The Odyssey

Aldous Huxley
Brave New World

Kazuo Ishiguro
The Remains of the Day

Ben Jonson
The Alchemist

James Joyce
Dubliners

John Keats
Selected Poems

Philip Larkin
The Whitsun Weddings and Selected Poems

Christopher Marlowe
Doctor Faustus
Edward II

Arthur Miller
Death of a Salesman

John Milton
Paradise Lost Books I & II

Toni Morrison
Beloved

George Orwell
Nineteen Eighty-Four

Sylvia Plath
Selected Poems

Alexander Pope
Rape of the Lock & Selected Poems

William Shakespeare
Antony and Cleopatra
As You Like It
Hamlet
Henry IV Part I
King Lear
Macbeth
Measure for Measure
The Merchant of Venice
A Midsummer Night's Dream
Much Ado About Nothing
Othello
Richard II
Richard III
Romeo and Juliet
The Taming of the Shrew
The Tempest
Twelfth Night
The Winter's Tale

George Bernard Shaw
Saint Joan

Mary Shelley
Frankenstein

Jonathan Swift
Gulliver's Travels and A Modest Proposal

Alfred Tennyson
Selected Poems

Virgil
The Aeneid

Alice Walker
The Color Purple

Oscar Wilde
The Importance of Being Earnest

Tennessee Williams
A Streetcar Named Desire
The Glass Menagerie

Jeanette Winterson
Oranges Are Not the Only Fruit

John Webster
The Duchess of Malfi

Virginia Woolf
To the Lighthouse

William Wordsworth
The Prelude and Selected Poems

W.B. Yeats
Selected Poems

Metaphysical Poets

SURFING
A Beginner's Guide

2nd Edition

ALF ALDERSON

Other Wiley Editorial Offices

John Wiley & Sons Inc., 111 River Street, Hoboken, NJ 07030, USA

Jossey-Bass, 989 Market Street, San Francisco, CA 94103-1741, USA

Wiley-VCH Verlag GmbH, Boschstr. 12, D-69469 Weinheim, Germany

John Wiley & Sons Australia Ltd, 42 McDougall Street, Milton, Queensland 4064, Australia

John Wiley & Sons (Asia) Pte Ltd, 2 Clementi Loop #02-01, Jin Xing Distripark, Singapore 129809

John Wiley & Sons Canada Ltd, 6045 Freemont Blvd, Mississauga, Ontario, L5R 4J3 Canada

Wiley also publishes its books in a variety of electronic formats. Some content that appears in print may not be available in electronic books.

Library of Congress Cataloging-in-Publication Data

Alderson, Wayne Alf.

Surfing: a beginner's guide/Wayne Alf Alderson. -- 2nd ed. p. cm.

Originally published: Arundel, West Sussex: Fernhurst Books, 1996.

ISBN 978-0-470-51654-6 (pbk.: alk. paper)

1. Surfing--Handbooks, manuals, etc. I. Title.

GV840.S8A395 2008

797.3'2--dc22

2007050387

British Library Cataloguing in Publication Data

A catalogue record for this book is available from the British Library

ISBN: 978-0-470-51654-6 (PB)

Typeset in the UK by Artmedia Press, London

Printed and bound in Italy by Printer Trento, Trento

This book is printed on acid-free paper responsibly manufactured from sustainable forestry in which at least two trees are planted for each one used for paper production.